GL

Th

ATHENS

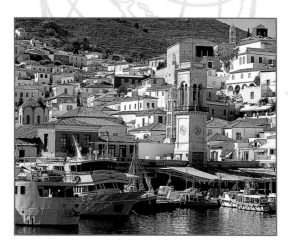

WILLIAM GRAY

NEW
HOLLAND

GLOBETROTTER™

First edition published in 2004
by New Holland Publishers (UK) Ltd
London • Cape Town • Sydney • Auckland
10 9 8 7 6 5 4 3 2 1

website: www.newhollandpublishers.com

Garfield House, 86 Edgware Road
London W2 2EA
United Kingdom

80 McKenzie Street
Cape Town 8001
South Africa

14 Aquatic Drive
Frenchs Forest, NSW 2086
Australia

218 Lake Road
Northcote, Auckland
New Zealand

Distributed in the USA by
The Globe Pequot Press, Connecticut

ISBN 1 84330 634 4

Although every effort has been made to ensure
that this guide is up to date and current at time
of going to print, the Publisher accepts no
responsibility or liability for any loss, injury or
inconvenience incurred by readers or travellers
using this guide.

Publishing Manager (UK): Simon Pooley
Publishing Manager (SA): Thea Grobbelaar
DTP Cartographic Manager: Genené Hart
Editor: Melany McCallum
Designer: Lellyn Creamer
Cover design: Lellyn Creamer, Nicole Engeler
Cartographer: Marisa Galloway
Picture Researcher: Shavonne Johannes
Proofreader: Anna Tanneberger

Reproduction by Fairstep (Cape Town) and
Hirt & Carter (Pty) Ltd, Cape Town
Printed and bound in Hong Kong by Sing Cheong
Printing Co. Ltd.

Front Cover: *Crowned by the Parthenon,
the Acropolis rises above Athens.*
Title Page: *This delightfully chaotic scene of
boats and waterfront houses greets day-trippers
to the Saronic Gulf island of Hydra.*

CONTENTS

MAKE THE MOST OF YOUR GUIDE

Reading these two pages will help you to get the most out of your
guide and save you time when using it. Sites discussed in the text are
cross-referenced with the cover maps – for example, the reference
'Map B–C3' refers to the Athens Map (Map B), column C, row 3. Use the
Map Plan below to quickly locate the map you need.

MAP PLAN

Outside Back Cover   Outside Front Cover

Inside Front Cover   Inside Back Cover

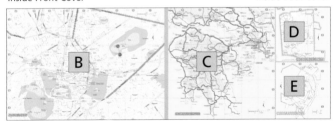

THE BIGGER PICTURE

Key to Map Plan

A – Metro and Railway

B – Athens

C – Peloponnese

D – Ancient Delphi

E – Ancient Eleusis

F – Piraeus

G – Nafplio

H – Ancient Olympia

Key to Symbols

⊠ — address   ⌐⊕ — e-mail address

☎ — telephone   ⊕ — opening times

⌐ — fax   ⓔ — entry fee

�■ — website   ⦿⦿ — restaurants nearby

Map Legend

motorway	▬▬▬	cable car	●━━━●
national road	▬▬▬	motorway	**Athinon**
main road	▬▬▬	main road	**Lenorman**
secondary road	▬▬▬	road	Akadimías
railway	┼┼┼┼	metro	Omónia ─Ⓜ─
route number	8	wall	▬▬▬▬
airport	✈ ✈	building of interest	Olympia Theatre ▢
city	ATHENS	church	△ Ágios Geórgios
major town	⊙Thebes	hotel	Ⓗ DRYADES
town	O Erithres	hospital	⊕
large village	◎ Asopia	post office	⊠
village	OPlataea	information cetre	ⓘ
place of interest	● Lykavitós	market	▢
ruin	⁂ Temple of Poseidon	bus terminus	⊕
cave	◉ Koutoúki	built-up area	▢
nature reserve and park	Parnassós National Park	library	📖
peak in metres	Mount Oros ▲ 532 m	ferry route	Ferry to Crete
water	∿		

Keep us Current

Travel information is apt to change, which is why we regularly update our guides. We'd be most grateful to receive feedback from you if you've noted something we should include in our updates. If you have any new information, please share it with us by writing to the Publishing Manager, Globetrotter, at the office nearest to you (addresses on the imprint page of this guide). The most significant contribution to each new edition will be rewarded with a free copy of the updated guide.

Above: *Athens is home to some 3.5 million people.*

ATHENS

Think 'Greece' and you may naturally think 'Greek islands'. The capital, Athens, was always going to have a fairly difficult time competing with those irresistible specks of holiday heaven. And it has not helped itself by developing a reputation for congestion and smog. After a day in this vibrant, fascinating city, however, you will soon realize why it is fast becoming a highlight every bit as appealing as Corfu or Lésvos.

Not only is Athens cleaning up its environmental and traffic problems, but it is also polishing its image as one of the world's most important historical cities. To sightsee in Athens is to romp through the ages. From the ancient ruins of the **Acropolis** to state-of-the-art developments for the **2004 Olympic Games**, Athens mixes old and new to form an exciting cocktail of architecture, culture and the arts. There are enough monuments, churches and museums to satisfy the most hungry of minds – while great shopping, fine dining and a buzzing nightlife will fulfil those other city-break 'essentials'.

Beyond Athens, the surrounding areas of Attica, Delphi, Epidaurus and Ancient Mycenae are just day trips away, and if you still find your mind wandering to those Greek islands, you can always hop on a ferry to the nearby **Saronic Gulf islands**.

Facts and Figures

• Greece occupies an area of over 500,000km² (193,000 sq miles), of which 131,900km² (50,900 sq miles) is land. Greater Athens covers 427km² (165 sq miles).

• The highest mountain in Greece is **Mount Olympus** at 2917m (9570ft), while the highest point in Athens is **Lykavitós Hill** at 277m (909ft).

• Greece has a **population** of around 11 million, with an estimated 3.5 million people living in Greater Athens. The next most populous cities are Thessaloníki and Piraeus which have 750,000 and 175,000 inhabitants respectively.

The Land

Climate

Athens has a Mediterranean climate which is characterized by hot dry summers and mild winters. Temperatures peak during July and August when the city can sizzle at over 40°C (104°F). There is little, if any, rain in summer – although snow is not unheard of in winter. The Peloponnese mountains often receive a heavy snowfall.

Flora and Fauna

Wildlife is perhaps not foremost in the minds of visitors to Athens although there are a few green oases. Some of the best places for city flora and fauna are **archaeological sites**. Kerameikós (*see* page 26) has a good show of spring flowers, while butterflies and lizards can also be seen here.

However, to better appreciate the flora and fauna in Greece you need to head out of Athens. Mount Párnitha National Park and Mount Pendeli support numerous species of birds, plus a good range of some of the country's 6000 native **wild flowers**, as well as **birds**. Coastal wetlands provide important habitat for grebes, ducks and other water birds, while a boat trip to the islands in the Saronic Gulf will likely be rewarded with a glimpse of **dolphins**.

History in Brief

Athens was inhabited by the end of the **Neolithic Age** (ca. 3500BC). Early settlers must have prized the Acropolis as an easily defended vantage point and by 1400BC, the Acropolis had become a **Mycenaean** fortress. Somehow, the citadel survived the Dorian invasions which coincided with the

Bird-watching
Over 380 species of birds can be found in Greece. Spring and autumn are the best times for bird-watching since these seasons coincide with annual migrations. Although Athens is not one of the country's birding hot spots, it's still worth looking out for kestrel, short-toed tree creeper, pipits, warblers and flycatchers at the Acropolis, the National Gardens and Lykavitós Hill.

Below: *Parts of Athens, especially protected archaeological sites like Areopagus Hill, are surprisingly green.*

Guide to the Gods
• **Aphrodite** (Venus): goddess of love; mother of **Eros** (Cupid).
• **Apollo**: god of music, poetry and healing.
• **Ares** (Mars): god of war.
• **Artemis** (Diana): goddess of hunting.
• **Athena** (Minerva): goddess of wisdom and guardian of Athens.
• **Demeter** (Ceres): goddess of earth and fertility.
• **Dionysos** (Bacchus): god of wine and merriment.
• **Hades** (Pluto): god of the Underworld.
• **Hephaestus** (Vulcan): god of the forge.
• **Heracles** (Hercules): god-hero famed for his Twelve Labours.
• **Hermes** (Mercury): messenger of the gods.
• **Hestia** (Vesta): goddess of the hearth.
• **Poseidon** (Neptune): god of the seas.
• **Zeus** (Jupiter to the Romans): supreme deity; father of the gods.

demise of Mycenae's great empire around 1200BC. The **Dark Ages** that followed, however, were all-consuming. Poverty and depopulation racked the region and it was not until 800BC that Athens emerged as the leader of a group of Attic city-states.

The city was governed by aristocrats who elected the chief priest, general and archon (civil ruler). In 560BC **Psistratos**, a former general, seized control of Athens. Succeeded by his son, **Hippias**, the dictatorship lasted half a century before **Kleisthenes** overthrew it. Peace prevailed until Athens attacked Persia, which duly retaliated. The Battle of Marathon in 490BC resulted in an amazing victory for Athens. In 480BC, however, **Xerxes**, son of the Persian king, Darius, returned with a formidable invasion force and **Themistocles**, the city's ruler, had little choice but to evacuate Athens which was duly razed to the ground. Fortunes once again reversed when Persia's navy was

Opposite: *Top god, Zeus, known to the Romans as Jupiter.*
Right: *A statue of Athena, the goddess of wisdom and guardian of Athens.*

destroyed by Themistocles' fleet at the **Battle of Sálamis**. Conflict with Persia reached crunch point when Athenians, Spartans and their allies defeated the great eastern empire at **Plataea**. Themistocles quickly commissioned new warships and defensive walls and set in place the **Delian League** (an alliance of 200 city-states that swelled Athens' army, navy and treasury in return for protection from the Persians).

In 461BC, the treasury was moved from Delos Island to Athens. **Pericles** (who ruled Athens from 461–429BC) launched his building programme, culminating in such marvels as the Acropolis temples. Athens embraced its Golden Age in a proactive flurry of science, art and culture. Big names included Pheidias, Herodotus, Socrates, Aristophanes, Sophocles and Euripides. In the 5th century BC, the basis of western culture was being forged in Athens. Sparta was turning green with envy and conflict was inevitable.

The **Peloponnesian Wars** (431–404BC) began with Sparta taking Attica. Pericles had planned for the likely danger of a siege and had strengthened the city walls, but he could not have foreseen the plague that decimated the city's population. Athens finally toppled following the naval defeat at Aegospotami. Sparta abolished the Delian League and introduced a brutal new regime. By 378BC, a public revolt had expelled the occupiers and Athens had set up a second Delian League.

In 338BC, **Philip II of Macedonia** defeated the Greeks and took control of the city-states. Following his assassination, his son, **Alexander the Great**, became king and the centre of Greek culture shifted from

Acropolis Timeline

447–438BC Building of the Parthenon.
438–432BC Decoration of the Parthenon.
437–432BC Building of the Propylaia.
421–406BC Building of the Erechtheion.
420BC Building of the Temple of Athena Nike.
AD267 Parthenon interior destroyed by fire.
361–343 Parthenon repaired.
6th century Parthenon and Erechtheion converted to Christian churches.
12th century Propylaia used as a palace.
1456 Parthenon converted to a mosque.
1640 Explosion in the Propylaia.
1686 Temple of Athena Nike destroyed.
1687 Explosion in the Parthenon.
1835 Restoration of Temple of Athena Nike.
1839–1863 Restorations of Erechtheion, Parthenon and Propylaia.
1975 onwards Restoration of the Acropolis Monuments.

Above: *The Temple of Hephaestus in the Ancient Agora.*

Athens to Alexandria, Rhodes and Pergamon. When Alexander died, Athens was left to a succession of his generals.

In 197BC the **Roman** army moved in. Although they sacked Corinth (146BC) and laid waste to the Ancient Agora and walls of Athens (86BC), they also built some fine monuments and the city once more became a major seat of intellect.

By now, Christianity was well afoot. Pagan Greek and Roman gods as well as cult festivals like the Olympic Games were banned and Christianity was established as the state religion in Greece.

In 395 **Goths** swept through Athens and devastated the place. Emperor Theodosius I died and the Roman Empire was divided into Latin west and Byzantine east. Christianity continued to spread during the Byzantine Empire. Classical schools of philosophy were replaced with Christian theology ones and the Parthenon became a cathedral. Generally, though, it was a rough time – Barbarians invaded, there were earthquakes, another plague and, in 1081, **Normans** stormed in, signalling the start of a series of invasions by Franks, Florentines and Venetians. In 1456, **Turks** invaded Athens, beginning nearly 400 years of Ottoman occupation which was only contested and resolved during the **War of Independence**. The secret Greek liberation movement, **Filikí Etaireía**, commenced the war on 25 March 1821. It ended in 1827 when the Turks lost in the **Battle of Navaríno**.

The following year **Ioannis Kapodistras** became the first president of Greece, but was assassinated in 1831. A monarchy was then established under **King Otto** of Bavaria but in 1862, **Revolution** drove the king from Greece. Greece then became a 'crown democracy' and Greek Orthodoxy was made the state religion.

In 1923 Greece failed to seize former territory from Turkey and the resultant **Treaty of Lausanne** involved the expulsion of over a million Greeks – many of whom returned to Athens.

World War II then struck and many Athenians died (mainly from starvation) during German occupation. Unrest perpetuated a bitter civil war that lasted until 1949. Many Greeks migrated to the United States, Canada and Australia. In 1967, right-wing army colonels (the Junta) launched a destructive **military coup** which was finally overthrown in 1974. A referendum abolished the monarchy and the socialist PASOK government of **Andréas Papandréou** was elected in 1981. In the same year Greece joined the **European Community** (EC).

Government and Economy

Greece has been a parliamentary republic with a president as head of state since 1975. The president and 300-member parliament have joint legislative power. Athens, which is part of the prefecture of Attica, entered the European Monetary Union in January 2002 when the drachma was phased out to make way for

---

Olympic Fortunes
By the end of the 1980s, Athens was one of Europe's most polluted and traffic-congested cities. But the following decade witnessed a turning point. A positive mood swept Athens in 1997 following the decision to award the city the 2004 Olympic Games. A new-found confidence have urged the capital to get its act together. A new international airport has been built; museums and monuments are being renovated, while traffic and pollution problems are being tackled head-on with new metro and tram systems, pedestrianization and tree planting. It may not herald another 'golden age' for Athens, but it will certainly add to the pleasure and excitement of visiting (or living in) this dynamic city.

Below: *The Greek flag flying above the Parliament building.*

Greek Orthodox Easter

Easter is the most important religious event in the Greek Orthodox calendar. At dusk on Good Friday, a bier decorated with flowers and containing an effigy of Christ is carried through the streets. Church services are held at midnight on Easter Saturday, followed by candle-lit processions, celebrations and feasting on Easter Sunday – traditionally a time for families to reunite.

Opposite: *A trio of local men relax on the island of Spetses.*
Below: *Greece is almost entirely Greek Orthodox in religion.*

the euro ( ). The country's economy has been improved through structural reform and a comprehensive programme of deregulation and privatization of the telecommunication, electricity, shipping and airline industries. Greece has the third highest Gross Domestic Product (GDP) growth rate in the European Union. Tourism is one of the biggest earners (with over 12 million tourist arrivals a year), while the majority of the workforce is employed in either services or industry. Unemployment remains stubbornly high at around 11%, although inflation dropped from 20% in 1990 to 3.6% in late 2001.

The People

Of a total population of 3.5 million, some 600,000 Athenians are immigrants – a number that continues to grow with new arrivals from Albania, the Balkans, the former Soviet Union and other parts of the world. Many Athenians are descended from families evicted from southwest Turkey during the 'population exchange' of 1923.

Religion

About 98% of the Greek population belong to the Greek Orthodox Church with the remainder being mostly Roman Catholic, Jewish or Muslim. Several religious festivals dominate the Greek year, the most important being Easter. In Greek culture, 'name days' (celebrating the saint after whom a person is named) are more important than birthdays. Also of great significance are weddings and funerals. Greeks are generally quite superstitious and believe in the 'evil eye' (bad luck brought on by envy) so take care not to be too effusive when complimenting things of beauty – especially newborn babies.

Art
Ancient Greeks endowed the world with incredible art and architecture that not only takes pride of place in many of today's

great museums, but also influenced several great creative minds and movements – from Picasso to the Italian Renaissance.

Architecture
Athens boasts an extraordinary range of architectural styles, from 5th century BC temples to 21st century AD sports complexes.

Temples are characterized by Doric, Ionic and Corinthian columns – the latter being the most elaborate with their leafy scrolls. Byzantine **churches** are scattered throughout the capital, tucked away like terracotta nodules in a modern conglomerate of shops and restaurants. Typically, they feature a central dome flanked by vaults with smaller domes at the corners and three apses to the east.

Literature
On the **literature** front, ancient poets like Alcaeus, Pindar and Sappho have contemporary counterparts in the form of Constantine Cavafy and two Nobel Prize laureates, George Seferis and Odysseus Elytis. Nikos Kazantzakis, author of *Zorba* and *The Last Temptation*, is the most renowned 20th-century Greek novelist.

Temple Terminology
Capital: top of a column, either simply or elaborately carved, depending on the temple's architectural order (Doric, Ionic or Corinthian).
Caryatids: statues of women used instead of columns.
Cella: innermost room or sanctuary.
Entablature: everything above the column capitals.
Metopes: sculptured panels on a frieze.
Pediment: triangular part crowning ends of temple.

Five Great Temples
1. The Parthenon, Acropolis
2. Temple of Olympian Zeus, Athens
3. Temple of Poseidon, Cape Soúnion
4. The Erechtheion, Acropolis
5. Temple of Aphaia, Aegina

The Acropolis
✉ Main entrance off
Dionysiou Areopagitou,
Pláka
☎ 210 321 4172,
210 321 0219,
210 923 8724
📠 210 923 9023
🖳 www.culture.gr/
2/21/211/21101a/
e211aa01.html
🕓 08:30–18:30 Mon–
Fri, 08:30–15:00 Sat–
Sun May–Oct; 08:30–
16:30 Mon–Fri, 08:30–
15:00 Sat–Sun Nov–Apr.
Full moon opening:
once a year in Sep.
Closed public holidays.
🚼 From main entrance
💰 Adults 12,
students 6, under 18
free; Sun between
1 Nov and 31 Mar free;
the ticket is valid for the
Archaeological Sites of
Athens (Acropolis site
and museum, Ancient
Agora, Theatre of
Dionysos, Kerameikós,
Olympieion, Roman
Agora)
M Akropoli

**The Acropolis
Museum**
🖳 www.culture.gr/
2/21/211/21101m/
e211am01.html
🖳 www.greekislands.
com/athens/acr_mus.htm

⚙ *See Map B–C5/D5*   ★★★

THE ACROPOLIS

The 'Sacred Rock', rising 90m (295ft) above the sprawling capital of Greece is a global icon of ancient culture. 'Acropolis' breaks down to *acro* (highest point) and *polis* (town) – but this says nothing of its achievements in architecture, nor its prime position as a place of worship and defence.

By climbing up to the Acropolis, you are following in the footsteps of the **Panathenaic Procession** when the residents of 5th century BC Athens marched up to the Acropolis and entered through the temple gateway of the Propylaia. To their left, stood a 9m (30ft) statue of Athena Promachos. To the right, in the Sanctuary of Artemis Brauronia, stood a huge bronze depiction of the Trojan horse. The procession then made its way to the **Parthenon** (*see page 17*).

The first entrance is the **Beulé Gate** (*see* opposite). Walk along the edge of the **Propylaia** (*see* opposite) to view the **Temple of Athena Nike** (*see page 16*) and then on to the Acropolis plateau which is dominated by the **Parthenon** and the **Erechtheion** (*see* page 18). In the southeast corner is the **Acropolis Museum** which houses statues and friezes (*see* opposite panel). The **New Acropolis Museum** (*see page 36*) will soon be located beneath the Acropolis.

Before leaving through the Beulé Gate, admire the impressive city views – Pláka and Monastiráki (north), Kolonáki and Lykavitós Hill (east), Philopáppou Hill (south), and Hill of the Nymphs (west).

See Map B–C5 ★★★

Left: *The Propylaia forms a monumental gateway to the Acropolis.*
Opposite: *Crowned by the Parthenon, the Acropolis rises above the streets of Athens.*

THE PROPYLAIA

Built between 437 and 432BC, the Propylaia was designed by Mnesikles to form a gateway to the Acropolis. The imposing temple-like structure was supported by rows of Ionic and Doric columns that channelled visitors through five doorways – the centremost of which led to the Panathenaic Way. To the left, a massive plinth once supported a statue of a charioteer. The north wing housed an art gallery, the Pinakothéke, which also served as a chamber where VIPs could rest after the long climb. Greek travel writer, Pausanias, recorded seeing paintings here around AD150. Later, the Propylaia was used as an archbishop's residence, Frankish palace and Turkish fortress.

The Beulé Gate

Discovered in 1852 by French archaeologist Ernest Beulé, this simple gateway between the ticket office and the Propylaia was built in AD267 to reinforce the Acropolis. Fragments of a choregic monument (*see* page 31) on the south slope of the Acropolis were used in its construction.

> **Acropolis Museum Star Exhibits**
> **The Moschophoros** (570BC): statue of a bearded man carrying a calf on his shoulders.
> **Rampin Rider** (550BC): horseman statue used as a dedication to Athena.
> **The Peplos Kore** (530BC): statue of a young woman (kore) wearing a peplos.
> **Mourning Athena** (460BC): relief depiction of the goddess clad in a peplos.
> **Parthenon frieze** (438–432BC): east section showing the gods Poseidon, Apollo, Artemis, Aphrodite and Eros.
> **The Caryatids** (420BC): original statues of the women that supported the roof of the south porch of the Erechtheion.

⊙ *See* Map B–C5   ★★★

Right: *The Temple of Athena Nike was the first Ionic temple to be built on the Acropolis.*

TEMPLE OF ATHENA NIKE

The history of this shrine to Athena Nike, the Warrior, is literally one of ups and downs. Built in 478BC from a design by **Kallikrates**, it was destroyed by Turks in 1687, reconstructed in 1835, dismantled and rebuilt in 1936, then taken down again in 2002. The latest restoration, using a titanium frame, should be complete by 2004.

The temple stands on a 9.5m (31ft) bastion and has four Ionic columns of 4m (13ft) high. Fragments of a frieze (a replica) depicting the Battle of Plataea (479BC) can still be seen, while the balustrade is adorned with a sculpture of Athena.

According to legend, King Aegeus held vigil at the temple, waiting for his son, Theseus, to return from Crete. Theseus had set out to slay the Minotaur, but on his return to Athens he forgot to signal his victory with a white sail. Devastated upon seeing a black one, King Aegeus threw himself off the precipice – immortalizing his name in the Aegean Sea.

Areopagus
Well-worn (and slippery) marble steps lead to the top of Areopagus (Hill of Ares) from just below the Acropolis ticket office. In ancient times, the supreme court held trials here for murder, treason and corruption. It was also the site from where St Paul delivered his sermon in AD51 (the text is inscribed on a plaque near the steps). Nowadays, tourists climb to the top for stunning views across the Ancient Agora and the rooftops of Athens.

See Map B–D5 ★ ★ ★

THE PARTHENON

One of the world's most famous ancient buildings, the Parthenon was designed by Kallikrates and Iktinos. Construction began in 447BC and finished in time for the Great Panathenaic Festival of 438BC. Dedicated to **Athena Parthenos**, the Virgin, it was built on the site of at least four earlier Parthenons.

As well as being a shrine to Athena, it has served a number of functions ranging from a treasury for the **Delian League** (*see page 9*) to a powder magazine for the Turks.

Apart from its roof, it was constructed entirely of Pentelic marble. Its design, from the 46 Doric columns to its base and steps, was intended to counteract the laws of perspective and create the illusion of perfect symmetry. Despite its estimated 13,400 blocks of marble, weighing up to 10 tons each, the Parthenon has no straight lines.

A statue of Athena stood in the east cella (inner sanctum), while the exterior of the temple was decorated with sculptures and friezes. The two pediments depicted the birth of Athena and her battle with Poseidon (only fragments remain following an attempt by Morosini to take them to Venice). Sculptures on the entablature showed battles between the gods and giants on the east side, the Athenians and the Amazons on the west, the Lapiths and centaurs on the south and the Battle of Troy on the north.

Parthenon Marbles
The Ionic frieze running 160m (524ft) along the exterior of all four walls of the cella portrayed the Panathenaic Procession – a remarkable scene of 400 humans and 200 animals designed in low relief by Pheidias. In 1816, **Lord Elgin** sold sections of these so-called Parthenon (or Elgin) Marbles to the British Museum (*see panel on page 10*).

The **New Acropolis Museum** (*see page 36*) has been specifically designed to incorporate the missing pieces, adding to international pressure for their return to Athens.

Below: *View of the Parthenon from the west.*

See Map B–D5   ★ ★ ★

THE ERECHTHEION

The Erechtheion (built between 421 and 406BC) is located on the most sacred site of the Acropolis. It was here that Poseidon and Athena are said to have fought over who should become patron of the city. Poseidon struck the ground with his trident to create the salt spring Klepsydra, while Athena germinated the first olive tree and claimed victory (an olive tree – though not the original – grows in the temple's western court).

The main temple was dedicated to both Athena Polias and Erechtheus Poseidon – the two principal gods of Attica. It takes its name from Erechtheus, a mythical king of Athens who was part man, part snake. His tomb was in the north porch – a particularly sacred spot fronted by six tall Ionic columns and a partly exposed roof and floor to reveal the marks left by Poseidon's trident.

This elegant building is famed for its caryatids (statues of women used as columns) on the south porch – the **Porch of the Caryatids**. Each one originally held a libation vessel – which suggests that they represented the priestesses, or *Arrephoroi*, who attended Athena. Four of the original caryatids are in the Acropolis Museum (see page 14) – the Erechtheion now has only replicas.

Among its many roles, the least auspicious was as a Turkish harem and toilet in 1463. It was almost completely destroyed by cannon fire during the War of Independence.

Restoration of the Acropolis Monuments

Although excavation and restoration on the Acropolis has been ongoing since 1835, it was not until 1975 that major interventions were imposed to counter problems caused by centuries of damage from earthquakes, fires, bombardment, vandalism and, more recently, atmospheric pollution. Modern, highly technical approaches to restoration involve dismantling the restored or unstable parts of each monument, removing sculptures for safekeeping and replacing them with exact cast replicas, reassembling dismantled sections using authentic materials, and rectifying errors made in previous restorations.

Below: *Used in place of columns, these graceful caryatids support the south porch of the Erechtheion.*

THE ERECHTHEION & ANCIENT AGORA

See Map B–C4 ★ ★ ★

ANCIENT AGORA

For some 850 years from 600BC, the Agora was the social, commercial, political and administrative heart of Athens. Markets, law courts, schools, a prison, libraries, theatres, workshops, temples and a mint crowded this hub of public life.

Above: *Tucked into a corner of the Ancient Agora site is the fine Byzantine church of Ágios Apóstoli.*

Near the main entrance, the **Altar of the Twelve Gods**, was where distances to all points in the Greek world were measured. Along the **Panathenaic Way** (that linked the Agora with the Acropolis) towards the centre you'll find the **Temple of Ares** and **Odeion of Agrippa** (auditorium). Bear right towards the **Bouleuterion** (council chamber) and **Metroön** (record office), beyond which lies the **Temple of Hephaestus** (or Theseion). This superbly preserved temple, which uses design trickery to create the illusion of perfection, was built in 449BC to honour the god of metalsmiths. It served as a church from AD1300 until 1834 when it became Greece's first archaeological museum.

Continue on to the **Tholos** (council headquarters), the **Middle Stoa** and the Stoa of Attalos. Recreated in the 1950s, 22 centuries after it opened in 138BC, the **Stoa of Attalos** replicates a typical arcade. Named after King Attalos of Pergamon, the original stoa housed 42 shops, as well as public latrines. Today it contains the **Agora Museum** which displays artefacts from this complex site. In the southeast corner of the Agora is **Ágios Apóstoli**, a church containing fine Byzantine frescoes.

Ancient Agora
⊠ Below the Acropolis
🖳 www.culture.gr/
2/21/211/21101m/
e211am02.html
🕓 daily, 08:00–19:00
May–Sep, 08:00–17:00
Oct–Apr
M Monastiráki, Thision

Agora Museum
⊠ 24 Adrianoú Street,
Monastiráki
☎ 210 321 0185
🕓 08:30–14:45 daily
(except Mon)
💰 €4

⚙ *See* Map B–E6   ★ ★ ★

Above: *The Temple of Olympian Zeus once boasted 104 columns.*

TEMPLE OF OLYMPIAN ZEUS

Measuring over 96m (315ft) long and 40m (131ft) wide, this was the largest temple ever built in Greece – dwarfing even the Parthenon. Dedicated to Zeus Olympios, it took several attempts, spanning some 700 years, to complete. Peisistratos began the process around 515BC, with Antiochus IV Epiphanes, King of Syria, making another attempt in 174BC. It was not, however, until the reign of Emperor Hadrian that the temple was finally finished in time for the Panhellenic Festival of AD132. It must have been a magnificent sight – 104 columns each measuring 17m (56ft) in height surrounding an inner sanctum in which stood a gold and ivory statue of Zeus.

Only 15 columns remain today, each one characterized by an elegant Corinthian capital that replaced simple Doric ones in 174BC in the course of the temple's protracted creation. One tumbled during a gale in 1852 and has been left where it fell.

Other excavations at the site have revealed the remains of the **Temple of Apollo Delphinios** (500BC), parts of the **old city walls** (479BC) and **Roman baths** (AD131–132).

Temple of Olympian Zeus
✉ Olympieion, Vas. Olgas, Zappeio, Syntagma (next to Hadrian's Arch)
☎ 210 922 6330
💻 www.culture.gr/ 2/21/211/21103a/ e211ca02.html
🕐 08:30–14:30 Tue–Sun
Ⓜ Akropoli

See Map B–E1   ★★★

NATIONAL ARCHAEOLOGICAL MUSEUM

This museum's priceless collections span the millennia, providing a comprehensive overview of Greek history and art.

The Cycladic style is represented by the **Harpist** (2800–2300BC) and a **female figurine** from Amorgós. There are also **Thíra frescoes** dated to 1500BC and a collection of **Mycenaean gold** and other artefacts from Ancient Mycenae. The most famous piece is the **Mask of Agamemnon** – a gold death mask dating from the 16th century BC. Other Mycenaean treasures include a **bronze dagger** depicting a lion hunt, and gold **Vafeió Cups** that were discovered on Crete. There are also Linear B tablets, gold seals and a boar's tusk helmet.

Following the demise of the Mycenaean civilization (ca. 1150BC), the museum picks up the trail of Greek art revival with magnificent vases from the Geometric period.

Some of the archaic sculptures include the **Soúnion** *Kouros*, the **Phrasikleia** *Kore*, the **Aristodikos** *Kouros* and the earliest known Nike dated to 550BC. There are also some beautiful funerary *stelae* from Kerameikós and a reduced copy of the **statue of Athena** from the Parthenon.

Memorable exhibits from the Hellenistic era include bronzes of *Poseidon* and the *Jockey* while the Roman period is represented by busts of key figures, such as Hadrian and a statue of Augustus. Other collections are dedicated to pottery, bronzes, Egyptian art and jewellery.

National Archaeological Museum
✉ 44 Patission Street, Moussio
☎ 210 821 7717
📠 210 821 3573
🖥 www.culture.gr/2/21/214/21405m/e21405m1.html
🖥 www.greekislands.com/athens/nat_mus.htm
📧 protcol@eam.culture.gr
🕐 12:30–19:00 Mon, 08:00–19:00 Tue–Fri, 08:30–15:00 Sat–Sun, Apr–mid-Oct; 11:00–17:00 Mon, 08:00–17:00 Tue–Fri, 08:00–15:00 Sat and Sun, mid-Oct–Mar
M Viktorias

Below: *The National Archaeological Museum contains a priceless collection of artifacts.*

Goulandrís Museum of Cycladic and Ancient Greek Art
⊠ 4 Neophytou Douka Street, Kolonaki
☎ 210 722 8321/3
📠 210 723 9382
🖥 www.cycladic-m.gr
⌨ info@cycladic-m.gr
🕐 10:00–16:00 Mon, Wed, Thu, Fri; 10:00–15:00 Sat; closed Tue, Sun and public holidays
💰 €3,50; students €1,80; archaeologists and archaeology students: free
🍴 Café in the courtyard
Ⓜ Evangelismos

GOULANDRÍS MUSEUM OF CYCLADIC AND ANCIENT GREEK ART

The simplistic, yet mesmerizing, marble figurines in this remarkable museum provide striking evidence of a culture that flourished in the Cyclades islands from 3200–2000BC. Opened in 1986 with a collection from the Goulandrí shipping family, the Museum of Cycladic Art contains over 300 objects from this little-known civilization. The most enigmatic exhibits on the first-floor are the **female figurines** (nude with arms folded over the belly) and rarer **male figurines**. **Cycladic pots**, including the mysterious 'frying pans', are also on display. Whether these were used as drums or receptacles for offerings to the dead, is still unknown.

The second floor houses the **Ancient Greek Art Collection** with displays of pottery, terracotta figurines, sculpture, coins and jewellery. Tucked away in a corner is a delightful amphora still covered in worm casts and oyster shells from when it lay, undiscovered, on the sea bed.

Below: *The Goulandrís Museum of Cycladic and Ancient Greek Art is world-renowned for its Cycladic figurines.*

The third floor has temporary exhibitions, while the fourth floor contains the **Politis Collection** with its fine ancient vases and bronze helmets. In 1992, the museum was extended into the adjacent neoclassical **Stathátos Mansion** which houses the Greek art collection from the Athens Academy.

See Map B–F4 | ★ ★ ★

BENÁKI MUSEUM

The former home of the Benákis family, this superb museum was founded in 1930 by Antónis Benákis, the son of a wealthy Greek merchant. Over 20,000 items, ranging from sculptures and paintings to jewellery and costumes, are arranged chronologically over four floors.

The ground floor covers prehistory to the late Roman Period, the Byzantine Empire and post-Byzantine centuries. Look out for **Cycladic figurines** (2600–2500BC), **Mycenaean jewellery**, Attic amphorae (ca. 700–750BC), **Corinthian vases** (7th–6th century BC), and gold jewels from the Hellenistic **Treasure of Thessaly**. Some of the most important legacies of ancient painting – the **El Fayum portraits** – are next. Named after the Egyptian oasis where they were discovered, these strangely hypnotic artworks date from the 3rd century AD. Intricate mosaics, illuminated manuscripts, and a stunning collection of **Byzantine icons** are also on display.

The first floor focuses on the development of Hellenism during the period of Ottoman rule as well as ecclesiastical art from the post-Byzantine period. There are also two lavishly wood-panelled rooms from an 18th-century mansion in Kozáni.

The second floor portrays culture, economy and society on the eve of the War of Independence. It also houses special temporary exhibitions and a popular café.

The third floor covers Independence and the formation of the modern Greek State and includes portraits of Greek heroes and some interesting memorabilia.

Above: *The Benáki Museum houses one of the city's most diverse collections of Greek arts and crafts.*

Benáki Museum
✉ Main building and N. Hadjikyriakos-Ghikas Gallery, 1 Koumbari Street and Vas. Sofias Avenue, Kolonaki
☎ 210 367 1000
📠 210 367 1063
🖥 www.benaki.gr
✆ benaki@benaki.gr
🕐 Museum, shop and snack bar: 9:00–17:00 Mon, Wed, Fri, Sat; 09:00–24:00 Thu; 09:00–15:00 Sun; Tue closed
🍴 A snack bar on the terrace of the neoclassical building overlooks the city
Ⓜ Lines 2, 3 (Syntagma and Evangelismos)

Above: *Restored in 1955, the Theatre of Herodes Atticus is used today for outdoor concerts.*

See Map B–C5/D5 ★★

THEATRES OF THE ACROPOLIS
Theatre of Herodes Atticus

Built between AD161 and 174, and named after the Roman consul of the time, this small theatre (also called the Odeion of Herodes Atticus) was originally enclosed by a cedar roof that allowed for all-weather performances. Following restoration in the mid-1950s, it is now a magnificent venue for the summer **Athens Festival** (*see* page 73) – an international extravaganza of concerts, theatre and ballet, with seating for around 5000. The theatre's impressive colonnade was once adorned with statues of the nine Muses. Along with many of Athens' monuments, it was badly damaged during the invasion of the Heruli in AD267.

Theatre of Dionysos

Carved from the southeastern flank of the Acropolis around 330BC, the Theatre of Dionysos was not only the first theatre built of stone, but it was also the birthplace of the Greek tragedy. Built on the site of a 6th century BC wooden theatre, it was the venue of the famous **Dionysia Festival** (*see* page 72) where great playwrights had their plays staged. The Romans, who used the theatre as a gladiatorial arena, increased the seating capacity to 17,000 in 64 tiers but only about 20 survive. The front rows were for VIPs. One seat, reserved for the priest, Dionysus Eleutherios, still bears griffins and lion's paws. The theatre also boasts a fine stage front depicting scenes from the life of Dionysos, the god of wine and merriment.

Theatre of Herodes Atticus
✉ Dionysiou Areopagitou Street, Makrigianni (southern slopes of the Acropolis)
☎ 210 323 2771, 210 323 5582
🕐 9:00–14:00, 18:00–21:00 daily
Ⓜ Akropoli

Theatre of Dionysos
✉ Agora area
☎ 210 322 4625
🕐 08:00–19:00 Tue–Sun April–June; 08:00–19:00 daily Jul–Oct; 08:30–15:00 Tue–Sun Nov–Mar
🖳 www.culture.gr/2/21/211/21101a/e211aa02.html
💰 €1.47

See Map B–B5/B6 ★★

HILLS TO THE WEST
Philopáppou Hill

This hill is the perfect vantage from which to admire the Acropolis, Piraeus and the Saronic Gulf. The path to the summit passes the Byzantine church of **Ágios Dimítrios Loumpardiáris**. It derives its name from an incident in 1656, when it fell under the sights of a Turkish cannon on the Acropolis. Before the weapon (known as Loumpárda) was fired, a bolt of lightning destroyed the weapon and the garrison commander.

At the summit is the **Monument of Philopáppos**. Built in AD114–16, it is decorated with a frieze showing Philopáppos arriving in Athens for his inauguration as Roman consul. The **Dóra Strátou Dance Theatre** (see page 72) is also on the hill.

Hill of the Pnyx

This was the meeting place of the *Ekklesia* (Democratic Assembly) in the 5th century BC. Among the statesmen who spoke here were Aristides, Demosthenes, Pericles and Themistocles. Today, the hill is used for son et lumière shows (see page 71).

Hill of the Nymphs

North of the Pnyx lies another pine-clad hill reaching 103m (338ft) in height. It is the site of the **Asteroskopeíon** (Observatory) which was built in 1842 on the site of a sanctuary to nymphs.

Below: *Yuccas, euphorbias and other vegetation on Philopáppou Hill.*

Kerameikós
✉ 148 Ermoú Street
☎ 210 346 3552
🖳 www.culture.gr/
2/21/211/21103a/
e211ca01.html
⏲ daily, 08:00–19:00
May–Sep, 08:00–17:00
Oct–Apr
M Thissio

🜨 *See* Map B–B3   ★★

KERAMEIKÓS

Named after the potters (*kerameis*) who once worked on the local clay deposits along the banks of the River Eridanos, Kerameikós contains the remains of two ceremonial entranceways. The most important was the **Dípylon Gate**, constructed in 478BC. Guarded by two towers and boasting a large courtyard, this was literally the front door of ancient Athens and marked the starting point of the Panathenaic Way to the Ancient Agora and Acropolis. Built around the same time, the **Sacred Gate** led west to Eleusis (*see* page 80) along the pilgrimage route of the Sacred Way.

Kerameikós is best-known, however, as the site of an ancient cemetery with burials dating from the 12th century BC. Many of Athens' elite and wealthy were buried along **The Street of the Tombs** where most of the remaining graves and monuments are found. These include some beautifully ornate *stelae* (relief sculptures) – the Stele of Demetria and Pamphile is particularly striking – as well as an imposing marble bull on the tomb of Dionysos of Kollytos, a rich Athenian treasurer. The original is in the **Oberländer Museum** near the site entrance – along with a collection of artefacts ranging from black-figure funerary vases to small terracotta toys from children's graves.

Opposite: *The extraordinary Tower of the Winds dominates a corner of the Roman Agora site. Each of its eight sides depicts a different wind.*
Below: *The Stele of Dexileos commemorates a young man killed in 394BC during the Corinthian War.*

See Map B–D4 ★ ★

ROMAN AGORA

Although much of this Agora lies hidden beneath Pláka, the remains of Athens' Roman civic centre are still worth a visit. Excavations have revealed a large building which consisted of a courtyard surrounded by stoas containing shops and storerooms.

One of the most visible remains is a monumental entranceway, the **Gate of Athena Archegetis**, built between 19 and 11BC. Other nearby buildings included the **Agoranomion** (dedicated to Emperor Augustus) and the **Vespasianae** – a 68-seat public latrine from the 1st century AD.

The octagonal **Tower of the Winds** was a multipurpose sundial, weather vane, water clock and compass designed by the astronomer Andronikos, ca. 150–125BC. Its name comes from the eight winds, personified in friezes, on each compass-orientated side of the tower. Standing over 12m (39ft) in height with a diameter of 8m (26ft), the tower once held a bronze triton weather vane. Beneath the friezes are metal rods which cast shadows across etched sundial lines. Scant traces of the water clock, in the form of a circular channel, can be seen inside the tower which, during the mid-18th century, was used as a retreat for Muslim dervishes.

In another corner of the site, **Fethiye Djami Mosque** was constructed in 1456 on the ruins of an early Christian church and is one of the few remaining buildings in Athens from the Ottoman occupation.

Roman Agora
✉ Monastiráki
☎ 210 324 5220
🖥 www.culture.gr/
2/21/211/21101a/
e211aa04.html
🕐 daily, 08:30–19:00
May–Sep, 08:00–17:00
Oct–Apr
Ⓜ Monastiráki

What Wind Where?
Although weathered by time and the elements, the frieze on the Roman Agora's **Tower of the Winds** still clearly depicts the following eight winds: **Boreas** (north), **Kaikias** (northeast), **Apeliotes** (east), **Euros** (southeast), **Notos** (south), **Lips** (southwest), **Zephyros** (west) and **Skiron** (northwest).

See Map B–E4/F4 ★★

SYNTAGMA SQUARE

For people-watching, you can't beat **Plateía Syntágmatos** (Syntagma or Constitution Square). In the square itself, you will see several lottery-ticket vendors and bread-ring sellers, while on the courtyard in front of **The Parliament** (*Voulí*), there is always a pair of evzone National Guards patrolling in front of the **Monument to the Unknown Soldier**. Even if you don't intend using the metro, **Syntagma Metro Station** is a quirky 'must-see' with its fascinating display of archaeological finds uncovered during the station's excavation.

The Parliament

Dominating Syntagma Square, the neoclassical Parliament building was built from 1836–1840 and originally served as a palace for King Otto. In 1935 it became the seat of the Greek parliament.

The building also houses the **Monument to the Unknown Soldier**. Etched with a relief of a fallen Greek warrior, the tomb is guarded round the clock by a pair of evzones. Dressed in the traditional uniform of the klephts (mountain fighters during the War of Independence), the evzones' exaggerated marching manoeuvres are as elaborate as their costumes of short kilts and pom-pom shoes.

Every hour, on the hour, the guard is changed, while at 11:00 on Sundays a full ceremony unfolds in front of the tomb.

Syntagma Metro
Well worth a visit even if you are not planning to take a train, Syntagma Metro is a veritable museum of Athenian history. Excavation of the underground station in the early 1990s turned into the country's biggest-ever archaeological dig. Artefacts and ruins dating from the classical period to the 19th century were uncovered. They included an aqueduct, bronze foundries, a late Roman bath complex, early Christian and Byzantine churches and a section of Amalias Street from the reign of King Otto. Although many of the finds are held at the university, the metro station contains a well-presented and informative display.

See Map B–F6	★ ★

KALLIMÁRMARO (OLD OLYMPIC) STADIUM

This magnificent marble stadium is just across Leoforos Konstantinou Road which skirts the southeast corner of the National Gardens. Measuring 204m (669ft) in length and 83m (272ft) in width, Kallimármaro Stadium (also known simply as Stádio) can hold up to 60,000 spectators in 47 rows of seats. It was the venue of the first modern Olympic Games on 5 April 1896 – but the athletic history of this site dates back much further.

The original Panathenaic Stadium was built here by Lykourgos around 330BC. Hadrian oversaw its first renovation in the 1st century AD when it was used for gladiatorial contests. However, it was the wealthy Roman benefactor Herodes Atticus who foot the bill for its later reconstruction (using Pentelic marble) in time for the Panathenaic games of AD144.

Over the centuries that followed, the stadium gradually fell into disrepair. Its graceful, curved tiers of marble seats were chiselled away for use in other buildings or to make lime. Fortunately, the 2nd-century geographer Pausanias described the stadium in his *Guide to Greece*, and it was this text that helped to inspire the design of today's replica.

2004 Olympics Mascots
Wearing the colours of the Greek sea and sun, Athena and Pheros, the mascots for the 2004 Olympic Games in Athens were inspired by a bell-shaped, terracotta Greek doll dating from the 7th century BC. Known as a *daidala*, the ancient artefact is held in the city's National Archaeological Museum (*see page 21*).

Opposite: *High-stepping evzones continuously parade in front of the Monument to the Unknown Soldier.*
Below: *The huge marble Kallimármaro Stadium was the venue for the first modern Olympics in 1896.*

Ágios Nikólaos Ragavás
⊠ Corner of Prytaneíou and Epichármou
🕐 08:00–12:00 and 17:00–20:00, daily

⚙ *See* Map B–D4   ★★

ANAFIÓTIKA

Snug against the Acropolis, Anafiótika is a tangle of narrow, largely car-free, streets hemmed in by whitewashed houses with balconies crammed with bougainvillea and bright pots of geraniums. It is a scene more reminiscent of a typical Cycladic village than a city centre. In fact, scratch the surface of this atmospheric neighbourhood and you'll discover that it was actually intended to be a little piece of the Greek islands. Dating from the 19th century, the houses were built by migrant workers from the island of **Anáfi** who evidently wanted to remind themselves of home. They were brought to Athens following Independence to construct King Otto's palace.

Anafiótika is bounded by two 17th-century churches – **Ágios Geórgios** to the south and **Ágios Simeón** to the north – as well as the Byzantine chapel of **Ágios Nikólaos Ragavás**.

Below: *One of the many churches in Anafiótika.*

Ágios Nikólaos Ragavás

A very popular wedding venue, this 11th-century chapel was built using marble columns and other remains of ancient buildings. Its bell was the first to ring out after liberation from the Turks in 1833 and the Germans in 1944.

ANAFIÓTIKA & PLATEÍA LYSIKRÁTOUS

See Map B–E5   ★

Left: *The Monument of Lysikrátous with the Acropolis looming behind.*

PLATEÍA LYSIKRÁTOUS

Erected around 335BC, the **Monument of Lysikrátous**, which dominates this square, is a fine and rare example of a choregic monument. These were built to honour winners of the annual choral festival held at the **Theatre of Dionysos** (see page 24).

Named after its wealthy sponsor, this elaborate domed structure, comprising six Corinthian columns and a finial of acanthus leaves, would originally have supported a bronze tripod. A frieze near the top depicts a battle between the theatrical god, Dionysos, and Tyrrhenian pirates. Below is an inscription which reads, 'Lysikrátous of Kikynna, son of Lysitheides, was choregos; the tribe of Akamantis won the victory with a chorus of boys; Theon played the flute; Lysiades, and Athenian, trained the chorus; Evainetos was archon'.

Many centuries later, the monument served as the library for a Capuchin friary in which Byron reputedly wrote part of his epic poem, *Childe Harold*, in 1810.

Monument of Lysikrátous
✉ Lysikrátous Square (corner of Lysikrátous and Vyronos streets, Pláka)
🖥 www.culture.gr/2/21/211/21101n/e211an04.html

Lord Byron (1788–1824)
Background: British poet.
Achievements: publication of *The Maid of Athens* and parts of *Childe Harold*, inspired by his visits to Athens.
Best known for: his poetry and as a high-profile campaigner for Greek Independence.

Right: *Statues of Athena, Socrates and Plato at the Athens Academy.*
Opposite: *Night-time view towards the Acropolis from Lykavitós Hill.*

See Map B–E3 | ★

Athens Academy
✉ 28 Eleftherios Venizelos Avenue
☎ 210 360 0207
Ⓜ Panepistímiou

University of Athens
✉ 30 Panepistímiou Street, Syntagma
☎ 210 362 0020
📠 210 360 2145
🖥 www.uoa.gr/ uoauk/uoaindex.htm
Ⓜ Panepistímiou

National Library of Greece
✉ 32 Panepistímiou Street, Syntagma
☎ 210 361 4413
📠 210 361 1552
📧 Vlahou@nlg.gr
🕑 09:00–20:00 Mon– Thu, 09:00–14:00 Fri and Sat
Ⓜ Panepistímiou

City of Athens Cultural Centre
✉ 50 Akadimías Street
☎ 210 362 1601, 210 363 0706
🖥 www. athens-culture.gr
🕑 09:00–13:00, 17:00–21:00, daily (except Sun evenings and Mon)

THE NEOCLASSICAL TRILOGY

Head north from **Syntagma Square** (*see* page 28) along Panepistímiou Street and you'll soon encounter a remarkable architectural trio on your right.

The first of these 19th-century neoclassical landmarks is the **Athens Academy** which was designed by Theophil Hansen and built between 1859 and 1887. Athena and Apollo stand atop Ionic columns, while statues of Socrates and Plato sit on either side of the steps leading to this exquisite building with its pediments crammed with yet more sculptures.

Next door is the **University of Athens**, another masterpiece of Pentelic marble with an Ionic colonnade and sculptures of the Sphinx, depicting wisdom. The **National Library**, designed like a Doric temple and having over half a million books, completes the trilogy.

Behind the trilogy, the **City of Athens Cultural Centre** has useful information on events and exhibitions.

See Map B–G3 ★

LYKAVITÓS HILL

Towering behind Kolonáki, this 277m (909ft) hill provides spectacular panoramic views over greater Athens. Those with the energy can walk to the top (a path climbs through cypress and pine trees and the trek should take about one hour). Alternatively, a much quicker funicular railway operates daily from Ploutárchou Street and departs every 10 minutes (less often during winter), 08:00–23:45.

The whitewashed 19th-century chapel of **Ágios Geórgios** dominates the summit of Lykavitós and looks especially dramatic when floodlit at night. Every Easter, it is the starting point for a candlelit procession that winds down the wooded slopes to the city below.

Surrounding the chapel are observation decks with mounted telescopes enabling you to zoom in on the Acropolis, the Temple of Olympian Zeus and other city landmarks visible from the hill. On a clear day (if the pollution and haze allow) you should be able to see as far as the Saronic Gulf and occasionally even the island of Aegina.

Lykavitós Hill has a restaurant and a couple of cafés, as well as the open-air **Lykavitós Theatre** (see page 71) where classical, jazz and rock concerts are held during summer.

Hill with a View
Lykavitós Hill is the perfect vantage from which to contemplate the geography of Athens. As you gaze out across the city from the summit of this distinctive, cone-shaped hill, it becomes apparent that Athens lies in a basin surrounded by low ranges to the north, east and west with the sea to the south. You get the impression of a concrete reservoir lapping at distant hills, creeping imperceptibly up their slopes and trying to find a gap through which to spread. In fact, that's exactly what this burgeoning city is doing. Greater Athens occupies an area of some 427km^2 (165 sq miles), but every year sees it spilling further into the surrounding region, known as Attica.

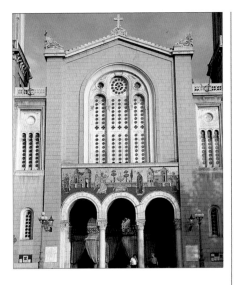

Above: *Modern mosaics adorn the entrance to the Mitrópoli.*

Five Great Byzantine Churches
1. Dáfní Monastery, west of Athens
2. Kaisarianí Monastery, Mount Ymittós
3. Kapnikaréa, Ermoú Street, Athens
4. Ágios Dimitrios Loumpardiáris, Philopáppou Hill
5. Ágios Apóstoli, Ancient Agora

Places of Worship

Panagía Gorgoepíkoös

Panagía Gorgoepíkoös or 'little cathedral' is just 7.5m (25ft) long by 12m (40ft) wide. What it lacks in scale, however, it more than compensates for with historical and architectural significance. Dating from the 12th century, this domed church (dedicated to the Madonna who Swiftly Hears) incorporates relief sculptures and other fragments of ancient and early Christian monuments.

✉ *Plateía Mitropóleos,*
🕓 *07:00–19:00 daily.*

Mitrópoli

Dedicated to Evangelismós Theotókou (the Annunciation of the Virgin), Athens Cathedral consumed marble from over 70 demolished churches during its construction from 1840–60. Adorned with a fine mosaic of the Annunciation above its entrance, the Mitrópoli covers an area of 40m (131ft) by 20m (66ft) and reaches a height of 24m (79ft). Inside are the tombs of two saints, Ágia Filothéi and Gregory V – both murdered by Ottoman Turks.

✉ *Plateía Mitropóleos,*
🕓 *06:30–19:00 daily.*

Kapnikaréa

Rising from a square in the middle of a busy shopping street, 11th-century Kapnikaréa was rescued from demolition in

1834 through intervention by King Ludwig of Bavaria. It was restored in the 1950s by the University of Athens and contains modern frescoes by Fótis Kóntoglou.

✉ Corner of Kapnikaréa and Ermoú,

🕙 08:00–14:00 Mon, Wed, Sat; 08:00–12:30, 17:00–19:30 Tue, Thu, Fri; 08:00–11:30 Sun.

Pantánassa

Believed to have been built in the 10th century, this is the 'little monastery', or *monastiráki*, which gave the area its name.

✉ East side of Plateía Monastiráki.

Russian Church of the Holy Trinity

Also known as Ágios Nikodímos, this 11th-century church was restored by Tsar Alexander II during the 1850s.

✉ 21 Filellínon,

🕙 07:30–10:00 Mon–Fri; 07:00–11:00 Sat and Sun.

Museums & Galleries
Greek Folk Art Museum

Showcasing everything from shadow puppets and festival masks to needlework and carving, the Greek Folk Art Museum also has some splendid masquerade costumes, including the famous masked goat dancer of Skyros.

✉ 17 Kydathineon,

🕙 10:00–14:00 Tue–Sun.

Kanellópoulos Museum

This museum, in a fine restored 1884 mansion, houses the extensive private collection of the Kanellópoulos family. It includes such treasures as Mycenaean figurines, Persian jewellery from the 5th century BC, Attic vases and Byzantine icons, as well as weapons, coins and portraits from the Hellenistic world.

✉ Corner of Theorías and Pános, 🕙 08:30–15:00 Tue–Sun.

> **Church Terminology**
> **Iconostasis:** screen, embellished with icons, that separates the altar from the rest of the church.
> **Katholikón:** main church of a monastery complex.
> **Narthex:** porch of a church.
> **Sacristy:** room where sacred vessels are kept.

Below: *The ornate neoclassical entrance to the Kanellópoulos Museum.*

New Acropolis Museum

Designed by Bernard Tschumi, the New Acropolis Museum will provide state-of-the-art displays of some of the world's most important antiquities. A glass gallery on top of the museum will showcase the **Parthenon Marbles** (including, it is hoped, the controversial sections that have been kept at the British Museum following Lord Elgin's 'acquisition' in 1801). The spectacular friezes will be reassembled using the same dimensions that they once occupied on the great temple itself. Near the base of the south side of the Acropolis, the museum will also provide views of the Parthenon, as well as displays of early settlements that were excavated and preserved during construction work.

Museum of Greek Popular Musical Instruments

Displays of numerous instruments dating from the 18th century feature here, including a collection of over 1200 from Cretan musicologist Phoebus Anogianákis. Headphones let you sample music from instruments as diverse as Greek goatskin bagpipes, a bouzouki and a lute. There is also a collection of church bells in the basement, while music recitals are sometimes held in the gardens.

⊠ 1–3 Diogenous, Pláka,

☎ 210 325 6198,

🕓 10:00–14:00 Tue, Thu–Sun, 12:00–18:00 Wed, closed Mon.

Museum of Traditional Greek Ceramics

Also known as Kyriazópoulos Folk Ceramic Museum (after the professor who donated many of the 20th-century jugs, jars and earthenware on display), this museum is located in an equally fascinating restored mosque. During its construction in 1759, the Turkish governor, Tsistarákis, needed lime for the mosque's stucco work, so he ordered one of the columns of the Temple of Olympian Zeus to be dynamited. He was exiled the same year.

⊠ 1 Areos,

🕓 09:00–14:30 Mon and Wed–Sun.

Centre of Folk Art & Tradition

Located at the home of folklorist Angelikis Hatzimichalis, this interesting centre conjures up images of the past through recreations of traditional Greek lifestyles.

✉ *6 Agelikis Hatzimichalis,*
🕐 *09:00–13:00, 17:00–21:00; 09:00–13:00 Sat and Sun.*

Frissíras Museum

With a mixture of permanent and temporary exhibitions, this museum houses a collection of 20th-century art by Greek and foreign artists.
✉ *3–7 Monís Asteríou,*
🕐 *11:00–19:00 Wed–Fri, 10:00–15:00 Sat and Sun.*

Jewish Museum of Greece

Tracing the history of the nation's Jewish community from the 3rd century BC, this museum includes shocking and moving insights into the Holocaust when nearly 90% of Greece's Jewish population was exterminated.
✉ *39 Níkis,*
☎ *210 322 5582,*
🕐 *09:00–14:30 Mon–Fri, 10:00–14:00 Sun.*

National Historical Museum

Prior to being opened as a museum in 1961, this neoclassical building was the site of the first Greek parliament. It now contains chronological exhibits tracing Greek history from Byzantine times to the 20th century. The War of Independence features prominently with displays of Byron's helmet and sword, as well as other weapons and costumes. Outside the museum is a statue of General Theódoros Kolokotrónis on horseback.
✉ *13 Stadíou Street, Syntagma,*
☎ *210 323 7617,*
🕐 *09:00–14:00 Tue–Sun.*

Byzantine and Christian Museum

Recently expanded and modernized, this museum showcases icons, sculptures, mosaics, woodcarvings, manuscripts, frescoes, ecclesiastical robes and jewellery

Opposite: *Dating from the Archaic Period, the Moschophoros, or Calf-Bearer, is one of the many fine exhibits in the Acropolis Museum.*

Theatre Museum
Celebrating Greek theatrical history from classical dramas to the present day, this small museum contains costumes, posters, props, a puppet theatre and displays on famous names, such as actress Melina Mercouri.
✉ 50 Akadimías Street,
🕐 09:00–15:00 Mon–Fri.

---

dating from the 4th–19th centuries. Occupying a graceful Florentine-style mansion that was home to the French Duchess de Plaisance in the mid-1800s, the museum was established in 1930. Two of the galleries are arranged as an early Christian and middle Byzantine chapel. Key exhibits include a 4th-century **funerary stele** showing Orpheus playing a lyre, a 7th-century **gold necklace** from the Mytilene treasure, and an 11th-century **marble slab** depicting three of the apostles. Among the stunning collection of **icons**, three of the most important are the 13th-century icon of *St George*, the 14th-century mosaic icon of the *Virgin and Child*, and the 18th-century icon of the *Virgin Nursing the Child*.
⊠ *22 Vas. Sofias, Kolonáki,*
☎ *210 721 1027,*
🕐 *08:30–15:00 Tue–Sun.*

Byzantine Art

Mosaics and frescoes in a Byzantine church have a symbolic arrangement from heaven to earth. The image of Christ Pantokrátor is always high in the dome. The Virgin is depicted in the semi-dome of the apse, while saints occupy the lower levels of the side walls.

Goulandrís Natural History Museum

Showcasing an extensive collection of plants, animals and minerals from Greece and further afield, this award-winning museum (opened in 1975) is located in one of Kifissiá's large villas.
⊠ *13 Levídou,*
🕐 *09:00–14:30 Sat–Thu.*

National Gallery of Art

A new wing was added to the National Gallery in 2000, while further hanging space is expected by 2004. There is a permanent European exhibition including five paintings by one of Greece's most renowned artists, **El Greco** (1541–1614). These include *Concert of Angels*, *St Peter* and *The Burial of Christ* which was bought in 2000 for US$700,000. Works by Brueghel, Cézanne, Goya, Picasso, Rembrandt and Van Dyck are also on display. Outside you can't miss the dynamic contemporary statue of *The Runner* by Kóstas Varotsos.

⊠ *50 Vas. Konstantinou, Kolonáki,*

☎ *210 721 1010,*

⊕ *09:00–15:00 Mon and Wed–Sat, 10:00–14:00 Sun.*

Spathári Shadow Theatre Museum

This quirky museum reveals the fascinating history of shadow puppet theatre – a popular folk art that has its roots in the Far East.

⊠ *22 Argonáfton, Maroússi,*

☎ *210 802 7185,*

⊕ *10:00–13:30, Mon–Fri.*

Other Places of Interest
Hadrian's Library

In its heyday around the 2nd century AD, Hadrian's Library would have been a grand affair measuring 120m (394ft) by 80m (262ft) and graced with 100 columns and a pool.

Although the ruins are not open to the public, you can still view part of the west wall from Areos Street.

⊠ *Areos, Monastiráki,*

☎ *210 322 9740.*

Hadrian's Arch

This triumphal arch was built in AD131 to mark the boundary between what Emperor Hadrian saw as 'old' and 'new'. An inscription on the Acropolis side reads, 'This is Athens, the ancient city of Theseus', while on the other side it states, 'This is the city of Hadrian, and not of Theseus.'

⊠ *Corner of Vas. Olgas and Amalias, Areos, Monastiráki.*

First Cemetery of Athens
Located near Kallimármaro Stadium and open 07:30–18:00 daily, the First Cemetery of Athens (not to be confused with the much older Kerameikós) is the final resting place for many famous names in recent Greek history. Tombs include those of German archaeologist Heinrich Schliemann, Nobel prize-winning poet Giórgos Seféris, benefactor Antónis Benákis, and actress and politician Melina Mercouri. Near the entrance there is a bronze memorial (*The Mother of the Occupation*) to the 40,000 Athenians who perished through starvation during World War II.

Below: *This impressive wall, built around AD132, is the most visible remains of Hadrian's Library.*

Wild Flowers
With over 6000 species of wild flowers, Greece has one of Europe's most spectacular floras. There are over 100 types of orchids alone. This diversity is due to the country's variety of habitats (ranging from coastal wetlands to mountains), as well as the fact that much of the land has escaped intensive agriculture. One of the country's best spots for wild flowers is the Peloponnese.

Below: *Exotic palms at the National Gardens.*

Parks and Gardens
National Gardens

When you simply need a shady bench on which to relax, the main entrances to the National Gardens are just a short stroll from the Parliament. Formerly known as the **Royal Gardens**, this 16ha (40-acre) park was ordered by Queen Amalía in the 1840s. Paths lead to ornamental ponds and quiet clearings adorned with modern statues. There are also children's play areas and a small **Botanical Museum**, while a café can be found off Irodou Attikou. In adjacent formal gardens to the south is the **Záppeion conference centre** – an impressive late 19th-century building that was the headquarters of the 1896 Olympic Committee. Also nearby is the **Presidential Palace** which was home to the Royal Family from 1890–1967 before becoming the official residence of the President.

⊠ *Between Vas. Olgas and Vas. Sofias, Syntagma,*
☉ *sunrise to sunset.*

Stréfi Hill and Areos Park

With the exception of the National Archaeological Museum, **Exárchia** (the northern district of Central Athens), lies off the main tourist track. Here, however, you will be able to experience the peaceful green havens of **Stréfi Hill** and **Areos Park**. The former has views of the Acropolis, while the latter is Athens' biggest park and contains wide tree-lined avenues and statues of heroes from the War of Independence.
⊠ *Exárchia.*

Left: *Olympic swimming pool, a venue for the 2004 Games.*

ACTIVITIES
Sport and Recreation

Since ancient times, Greeks have been more than a little keen on sport – something that is set to receive a huge boost in the wake of the **2004 Olympic Games**.

In Athens, residents and visitors can enjoy a number of recreational activities. **Jogging** is popular around the maze of paths in the National Gardens, around Kallimármaro Stadium and, if you feel like a challenge, up Lykavitós Hill. The **Athens Marathon** provides the opportunity to run along the original marathon route. It takes place twice a year and details can be obtained from SEGAS.

A number of centres within the coastal resort areas offer a variety of water sports such as **diving**, **sailing**, **waterskiing** and **windsurfing**. **Fishing** is also popular, especially during summer and autumn, and boats and fishing tackle can be found in most coastal villages.

Swimming is limited to hotel pools and the public pool opposite the Zappeion (otherwise head for the coastal resorts between Piraeus and Vouliagméni and

---

Running
Athens Marathon
💻 www.athensmarathon.com
SEGAS
✉ Syngrou 137
☎ 210 935 9302
💻 www.segas.gr

Diving
Aegean Dive Centre
✉ 53 Zamanou, Glyfada
☎ 210 894 5409

Sailing
Sailing Federation
✉ 15A Xenofondos Street, Athens
☎ 210 323 5560

Waterskiing
Vouliagméni Naval Club
✉ Vouliagméni Bay
☎ 210 896 2416

The Vitoratos School
✉ Varkiza Beach
☎ 210 897 2412

Windsurfing
Hellenic Windsurfing Association
✉ 7 Filellinon Street
☎ 210 323 0068

Fishing
Amateur Anglers and Maritime Sports Club
✉ Moutsopoulou Quay (Akti), Pireaus
☎ 210 451 5731

Pireaus Central Harbour Master's Office
☎ 210 451 1311

the islands of the Saronic Gulf). The best **beaches** are located along the beach-resort belt near Glyfada, south of Athens. Some of the pay beaches, such as the ones at Voula, Vouliagméni and Varkiza, hire out **tennis** and **volleyball** courts. **Tennis** facilities can also be found at Glyfada Athletic Club while **tenpin bowling** takes place at the Athens Bowling Centre.

Glyfada Golf Club has an 18-hole **golf** course as well as other facilities such as changing rooms, a restaurant, bar and golf shop. Rentals and lessons available.

Ipethrios Zoi (Outdoor Life) is a non-profit **hiking** club. They organize outings every weeked at minimal cost and anyone is welcome to join them. No special equipment is needed except good wallking shoes and a rucksack.

Dolphin Watching
The sea off southern Greece is home to several species of cetacean, including bottle-nose, common and striped dolphins, which may be sighted during a cruise in the Saronic Gulf (for cruise operators see page 49).

Fun for Children
The Museum of Greek Children's Art
This museum exhibits paintings inspired by an annual children's competition. It hosts regular art workshops for young-

---

Tennis
✉ Alipedou Voulas
☎ 210 895 3248

✉ Vouliagméni Beach
☎ 210 896 0906

✉ Varkiza Beach
☎ 210 897 2102

Glyfada Athletic Club
✉ Fivis and Metaxa streets
☎ 210 894 3800

Tenpin Bowling
Athens Bowling Centre
✉ 177 Oktovriou-Patission
☎ 210 867 3645

Golf
The Glyfada Golf Course and Club
✉ 15 Panopis, Glyfada (12km out of Athens)
☎ 210 894 6875/20
🖥 www.glyfadagolf.gr

Hiking
Ipethrios Zoi
✉ 9 Vas. Sofias
☎ 210 361 5779

sters and there is even a room where children can create artworks with the crayons and paper provided.

The Hellenic Children's Museum

This museum is a non-profit educational and cultural foundation with plenty of interactive displays and activities to keep children entertained for hours. Highlights include the 'grandmother and grandfather room' (a reconstructed room of an old Athenian house where children can dress up in period costumes) and a reconstruction of the new Athenian metro system.

The Fun Train

Ideal for families with young children (and big kids too), the **Fun Train** operates daily during the summer, linking all the main sites between Syntagma and the Acropolis.

Suggested Itineraries

One Day

With limited time, your main priorities have to be the **Acropolis** (*see* page 14) and **National Archaeological Museum** (*see* page 21). Intersperse these with a meal at a taverna in Pláka, a browse through the **Monastiráki flea market** (*see* page 53) and a quick stop at the **Parliament** (*see* page 28) to watch the changing of the guards.

Two Days

Stroll the **Ancient and Roman Agoras** (*see* pages 19 and 27), visit the **Tower of the Winds** (*see* page 27) and have coffee in the square beneath the Mitrópoli (Cathedral). Delve into the treasures of the **Benáki Museum** (*see* page 23) and enjoy

---

Museum of Greek Children's Art
✉ 9 Kodrou, Pláka
☎ 210 331 2621
📠 210 721 8919
🕓 10:00–14:00 Tue–Sat, 11:00–14:00 Sun
💰 free
M Syntagma

Hellenic Children's Museum
✉ 14 Kythatheneon Street, Pláka
☎ 210 331 2995/6
🖥 www.athens-culture.gr/english/sections/sect12.htm
✆ hcm@compulink.gr
🕓 09:30–13:30 Mon and Wed, 09:30–13:30 and 17:00–20:00 Fri, 10:00–13:00 Sat and Sun
💰 free
M Syntagma

Fun Train
☎ 275 209 7856
📠 275 202 9134
🖥 www.trenaki.gr
✆ trenaki@otenet.gr
🕓 11:00–19:00 daily in summer

Opposite: *The Tower of the Winds in the Roman Agora, with the Acropolis looming behind.*

Sightseeing in Athens

Athens is a walker's city. Its main sites are concentrated near the centre and, on foot, you will get to meet its people – from street vendors selling bread rings to market traders hawking old coins. See the sites, peruse the museums and shop for curios – but, above all, take your time. No visit to Athens would be complete without an hour or two day-dreaming at the top of Lykavitós Hill or a long, lazy lunch at a taverna.

lunch in the museum's restaurant overlooking the **National Gardens** (*see* page 40). Visit the **Goulandrís Museum of Cycladic and Ancient Greek Art** (*see* page 22) and the **Byzantine and Christian Museum** (*see* page 37). Go window-shopping in Kolonáki before taking the funicular railway up **Lykavitós Hill** (*see* page 33) to watch nightfall over Athens.

Three Days

Spend a quiet couple of hours in the ancient and atmospheric cemetery of **Kerameikós** (*see* page 26) before walking to the ancient **theatres of the Acropolis** (*see* page 24) and on towards the **Temple of Olympian Zeus** (*see* page 20) and the **Old Olympic Stadium** (*see* page 29). Spend the afternoon on a tour (or drive yourself) to **Cape Soúnion** (*see* page 79) to watch the sunset at the **Temple of Poseidon**.

Opposite: *Shops are filled with a variety of memorabilia in preparation for the Olympic Games.*
Below: *Flying Dolphin ferry docked at Aegina.*

Five Days

Spend a morning at **Moní Kaisarianí** nestled in pine forest on the slopes of **Mount Ymittós**, followed by an afternoon exploring the maze of streets in Pláka's Anafiótika quarter and shopping for souvenirs. On the next day hire a car or join an

organized tour to the **Peloponnese** (*see* page 83), visiting the canal and ancient remains at **Corinth**, the historic coastal city of **Nafplio** and the extraordinary archaeological sites of **Epidaurus** and **Ancient Mycenae**.

One Week or More

Visit some of Athens' smaller, lesser-known museums, churches and galleries; take a day trip to the spectacular sanctuary at **Delphi** (*see* page 81); catch a ferry from Piraeus and island-hop between Hydra, Spétses and other islands in the **Saronic Gulf** (*see* page 82); hire a car and tour Marathon, Rámnous and other little-visited archaeological sites in Attica, or spend two or three days in the western Peloponnese exploring Ancient Olympia and the beautiful Adriatic Coast.

Walking Tours

The best way to take in the major sites of Athens is on foot. Not only are many of the star attractions concentrated in a relatively compact area, but they are also being linked by an ambitious 4.4 million pedestrianization project.

The overriding factor to take into account before you hit the sightseeing trail is the time of day. Summer in Athens can be oppressively hot, so it's best to visit archaeological sites first thing in the morning before retreating to a museum when temperatures start to soar. Early birds will also catch the best light for photography and miss the large tour groups. Another reason to go sooner rather than later is that many sites and state-run museums close early afternoon.

Sightseeing essentials include comfortable shoes with good grip (ancient marble surfaces tend to be slippery and riddled with potential ankle-twisters), sunhat and sunscreen, camera and plenty of film (*see* side panel).

Photography

The best light for photographing ancient sites and general city scenes is early morning or late afternoon when low-angle sunlight accentuates shadows and enriches colours and textures. Scenes can become quite 'flat' and washed-out under the harsh midday sun, although this may be the only time for taking shots in narrow streets which are otherwise in deep shadow. Remember always to ask permission when photographing local people (unless, of course, your subject matter is the evzone guards on parade outside the Parliament building). Taking pictures inside monasteries and many churches is forbidden and you will not be allowed to use a tripod or flash inside museums. Film is widely available in tourist shops across Athens.

Don't worry about the possibility of getting lost in Athens. As along as you don't stray too far off the beaten track you should always be able to get a bearing on the Acropolis, or distinctively shaped Lykavitós Hill. Most Athenians speak some English and will usually be only too happy to point you back in the right direction.

Of more potential concern to the visitor is the stress of coping with the city's traffic, noise and pollution. The trick here, is to plan a modest bout of sightseeing each day, with 'quiet time' allocated in the parks and gardens or at a taverna, and to inter- sperse city days with excursions further afield. The metro, for example, can whisk you to Piraeus where ferries depart for the Saronic Islands, while organized coach tours regularly ply routes to Cape Soúnion, Delphi and the Peloponnese.

Exploring Kolonáki and Lykavitós

Nestled beneath the southern slopes of Lykavitós Hill, the district of Kolonáki oozes style. Its streets are lined with chic designer boutiques, pavement cafés and trendy bars. This is the place to go window-shopping or to sip *frappé* (iced coffee) alongside afflu- ent Athenians. That's not to say, however, that Kolonáki lacks any cultural interest. Far from it. The museums in this area include some of the city's finest, while the views from Lykavitós Hill are unrivalled.

Plateía Kolonakíou lies at the heart of this fashionable quarter. Named after the ancient column (*kolonáki*) that was found here, the square is tucked away down a side street leading off Vas. Sofias. This wide avenue has the so-called 'museum mile',

The Northern Suburbs
Hemmed in by hills to the east and west and the Saronic Gulf to the south, modern Athens has little alternative but to spread northwards. The metro is probably the quickest way to reach the city's northern suburbs. Stop at Irini for the **Olympic Stadium** (*see* page 75) at Maroússi for the **Spathári Shadow Theatre Museum** (*see* page 39) and at Kifissiá for the **Goulandrís Natural History Museum** (*see* page 38).

Kifissiá, a leafy suburb favoured by the wealthy ever since Herodes Atticus had a villa built here, can be explored in one of the horse-drawn carriages waiting by the metro station. Nearby is **Mount Pendeli**, site of a monastery founded in 1578, as well as the ancient quarries from which the famous Pentelic marble was cut for the Parthenon.

beginning with the **Benáki Museum** (*see* page 23) and continuing east with the **Goulandrís Museum of Cycladic and Ancient Greek Art** (*see* page 22), the **Byzantine and Christian Museum** (*see* page 37), the **War Museum** (*see* side panel) and, finally, the **National Gallery of Art** (*see* page 38). Don't expect to notch up the entire mile in one session. The first two museums are particularly outstanding and easily warrant a day between them.

Exploring Exárchia

Along with the Acropolis and Ancient Agora, the **National Archaeological Museum** (*see* page 21) is one of the city's must-sees. Next door to the museum is the **Polytechnic**, from where it's a short stroll along Stournari Street to reach **Plateía Exarchéion** – a lively area lined with bars and cafés that are popular with students. If, however, it's peace and solitude that you seek, **Stréfi Hill** and **Areos Park** (*see* page 40) are not far off. Several theatres are dotted around this area, as well as in the neighbouring districts of Vathi and Omónia. The **National Theatre** (*see* page 72) is just off **Plateía Omónias** (a traffic-clogged square that is being redeveloped to restore some of its former grandeur). Walk south from here down Athinas Street towards the Acropolis and you'll pass the **Town Hall** and **Central Market** (*see* page 53) before entering the district of Monastiráki.

> **War Museum**
> Difficult to miss with its display of fighter aircraft and military hardware outside the entrance, the War Museum traces battles, weaponry, armour, uniforms and strategies from Mycenaean times to World War II. Scale models depict battle scenes and fortified towns, such as Nafplio, while paintings and prints portray leaders from the War of Independence and evocative scenes from the two world wars.
> ✉ Corner of Vas. Sofías and Rizári Ilísia
> ⊕ 09:00–14:00 Tue–Sun

Below: *Military aircraft outside the War Museum.*

Byzantine Icons
Icon painters are concentrated in the Pláka area of Athens – especially in the streets just south of Plateía Mitropóleos. Some artists still use traditional materials (egg-based tempera on wood). Saints can be painted to order – you just need to supply a photograph for the artist to work from.

Exploring Pláka and Monastiráki

You could spend days delving into these historic districts north of the Acropolis.

About 1km (0.6 mile) west of Plateía Monastiráki (near Thissio metro station) is the ancient cemetery of **Kerameikós** (*see* page 26). To the east is the **flea market** (*see* page 53), **Hadrian's Library** (*see* page 39), the **Roman Agora** (*see* page 27) and **Anafiótika** (*see* page 30) – a maze of old houses tucked up against the Acropolis. Nearby is **Plateía Lysikrátous** with its intriguing monument (*see* page 31). The triumphal **Hadrian's Arch** (*see* page 39) is just a short distance to the southeast and leads to the mighty **Temple of Olympian Zeus** (*see* page 20). Strolling between these landmarks, you will encounter several **churches** and **museums** – all worth a visit if you have the time!

Exploring Syntagma

Lying at the hub of this city-centre district to the northeast of Pláka is **Plateía Syntágmatos** (*see* page 28). With its modern metro station, fountains and seats, the square is a popular meeting place for locals and tourists alike.

Venturing from the square, you can delve into the maze of paths that thread through the tranquil **National Gardens** (*see* page 40) or take in some of Athens' architectural gems – the **Academy**, **University** and **National Library** (*see* the Neoclassical Trilogy, page 32), and the **Záppeion** exhibition hall and **Kallimármaro Stadium** to the south. And, of course, you are never far away from a museum.

Below: *The remaining Corinthian columns of the Temple of Olympian Zeus.*

Organized Tours

The most popular half-day tours from Athens are **Athens Sightseeing** (a coach tour pointing out the major sites with stops at the Acropolis and the Temple of Olympian Zeus), **Athens by Night** (the son et

lumière, followed by a meal at a taverna with folk dancing), **Cape Soúnion** (usually an afternoon coach tour to the site of the famous Temple of Poseidon, *see* page 79) and **Ancient Corinth** (a whistle-stop tour of the canal and archaelogical site, *see* page 83).

Full-day tours (and longer) are available to **Ancient Mycenae** (*see* page 83), **Epidaurus** (*see* page 83), **Ancient Olympia** (*see* page 83) and **Delphi** (*see* page 81), as well as cruises to the **Saronic Gulf islands** (*see* page 82).

Hotel reception areas and the tourist office are good places to pick up brochures advertising any of the above. Major tour companies in Athens, include **CHAT**, **GO Tours**, and **Key Tours**.

Hop-In Sightseeing operates buses on set routes which you can join or leave at various stops. There are longer stops at the Acropolis and National Archaeological Museum.

The **City of Athens** hosts free walking tours of the city's main sites while the **Panhellenic Guides Federation** can organize private tours to selected archaeological sites around the city. **Rania Vassiliadou** also provides a guiding service.

Above: *The National Library – one of the impressive buildings in the so-called Neoclassical Trilogy.*

CHAT
✉ 9 Xenofontos
☎ 210 322 3137

GO Tours
✉ 20 Athanassiou
☎ 210 921 9555

Key Tours
✉ 4 Kalirois
☎ 210 923 3166

Hop-In Sightseeing
✉ 29 Zanni, Piraeus
☎ 210 428 5500
🖥 www.hopin.com

The City of Athens
☎ 210 323 1841
🕘 10:30 every Sunday and second Saturday of the month

The Panhellenic Guides Federation
☎ 210 322 9705

Rania Vassiliadou
☎ 210 940 3932

Above: *Souvenir shops line the streets of Spétses.*

Shopping

Athens is a shopper's paradise. You can buy virtually anything – from a plastic, glow-in-the-dark Parthenon to an exquisite piece of designer jewellery. The focus for 'retail therapy' is Ermoú Street (Syntagma) – particularly if you are on the lookout for a new pair of shoes. Designer fashion victims should head for the boutiques in Kolonáki, Kifissiá and Maroússi. Elite jewellers are strung along Voukourestíou, off Akadimías, while sacks of olives, spices and nuts can be found at the Central Market. For souvenirs, your best bet is Pláka or Monastiráki. Greek music is in good supply at the **Virgin Megastore**, ✉ 7 Stadíou, Syntagma, and **Metropolis**, ✉ 64 Panepistimíou, Omónia, while English-language books can be found at **Eleftheroudakis**, ✉ 17 Panepistimíou. If a newspaper is all you are after, check out one of the many *periptera* (kiosks) dotted around the city.

Pláka and Monastiráki

Pláka and Monastiráki are a magnet for locals and visitors in search of food, drink, nightlife and shopping. The most famous shopping venue is the local flea market (see page 53) while on the nearby streets of Adrianoú and Pandrósou there are shops crammed with imitation black-figure vases, t-shirts, postcards and other curios.

One of the best all-round shopping streets is **Ermoú** (named after Hermes, patron of commerce) which runs from Monastiráki towards Syntagma Square. Partly pedestrianized, its shops offer complete 'retail therapy' – from shoes and leather goods to clothes and jewellery.

Kolonáki

Kolonáki is also abuzz with shoppers. Most of the city's top **designer boutiques** are located around Kolonáki Square or streets leading from it, while exclusive **jewellers** are concentrated on Voukourestiou (off Akadimías). You will also find **souvenir shops** near the funicular railway station at the top of Ploutarchou Street.

Shops

Some of the shopping highlights include:

Acropolis Rugs

Acropolis has a wide selection of traditional Greek *floccati* (sheepswool rugs).
✉ *31 Voulis, Pláka,*
☎ *210 322 4932.*

Benáki Museum Gift Shop

Great range of books, plus some tempting replicas of ancient artefacts.
✉ *1 Koumbari, Kolonáki,*
☎ *210 362 7367.*

Cellier

Good range of Greek wines and liquers.
✉ *1 Kriezotou, Syntagma,*
☎ *210 361 0040,*
🖳 *www.addgr.com/wine/cellier*
✆ *cellier@genkacomm.gr*

Centre of Hellenic Tradition

Excellent selection of traditional handicrafts, including carvings and paintings.
✉ *36 Pandrosou, Monastiráki,*
☎ *210 321 3023,*
🕑 *10:00–19:30, daily.*

Christakis

Well-known and exclusive tailor shop. Choose from dozens of rolls of fabric for that special handmade shirt.

What to Buy
Food and drink: olive oil, honey, ouzo, retsina.
Souvenirs: worry beads, copper coffee pots, icon paintings, museum replicas.
Goods: ceramics, rugs, leather, gold jewellery.

Below: *Chic and sophisticated, Kolonáki is renowned for its designer boutiques.*

✉ *5 Kriezotou, Syntagma,*
☎ *210 361 3030.*

Hellenic Folk Art Gallery

Broad range of traditional handicrafts, including beautiful handmade carpets, kilims, tablecloths and tapestries, with proceeds going to the National Welfare Organization.
✉ *6 Ipatias Street (corner of Apollonos and Ipatias), Pláka,*
☎ *210 325 0524,*
🕓 *09:00–20:00 Tue–Fri, 09:00–15:00 Mon and Sat.*

Ilias Lalaounis

World-renowned jewellers creating exquisite pieces inspired by Greek and other cultures.
✉ *6 Panepistimíou, Kolonáki,*
☎ *210 361 1371.*

Martinos

Antiques from Greece and further afield, including icons, glassware and furniture.
✉ *50 Pandrosou, Monastiráki,*
☎ *210 321 2414.*

Miseyiannis

Greek coffee and everything you need to make that authentic brew.
✉ *7 Leventi, Kolonáki,*
☎ *210 721 0136.*

Museum of Cycladic Art Shop

Stunning range of replica Cycladic figurines.
✉ *4 Neofitou Douka, Kolonáki,*
☎ *210 724 9706.*

Spiliopoulos

Shoes galore with plenty of top brands, often at bargain prices.
✉ *63 Ermoú Street, Syntagma,*
☎ *210 322 7590.*

Stavros Melissinos

The famous poet and sandal maker of Athens.
✉ *89 Pandrosou, Monastiráki,*
☎ *210 321 9247,*
💻 *www.athensguide.com/poet.html.*

Below: *Looking for bargains at the flea market in Monastiráki.*

Thiamis

Beautiful, hand-painted icons. Your patron saint can be painted to order.
⊠ *12 Apollonos, Pláka,*
☎ *210 331 0337.*

Zolotas

Internationally acclaimed jewellers specializing in replicas of ancient Greek museum pieces.
⊠ *9 Stadíou, Syntagma,*
☎ *210 331 3320.*

Markets
Monastiráki flea market

A bargain-hunter's paradise with dozens of stalls selling everything from glassware, furniture and copper pots to oddities like an antiquated diving helmet or gramophone. Antiques, collectables and furniture feature strongly.
⊠ *Centred on Plateía Avissynías, Monastiráki,*
🕐 *daily, but busiest from 07:00–15:00 on Sun.*

Central Market

The Central Market is a fascinating place to wander around – even if you're not interested in buying any of the vast range of meat and seafood on sale. On nearby streets you will find stalls piled high with nuts, spices, olives, fruits, vegetables and cheeses.
⊠ *Athinias and Evripidae streets, Athinas, Omónia,*
🕐 *07:00–15:00 Mon–Sat.*

Piraeus flea market

As well as the usual junk and bric-a-brac stalls, there are also shops selling antiques, jewellery and other collectable items.
⊠ *Centred on Alipedou, behind the metro station,*
🕐 *07:00–14:00 Sun.*

Above: *The Central Market in Athens offers everything from fresh fish and meat to nuts and dried fruit.*

Customs
Duty-free restrictions no longer apply within the EU. For non-EU citizens, the duty-free allowance includes 1 litre of spirits or two litres of wine; 200 cigarettes or 50 cigars and 50g of perfume.

Above: *The luxurious Grande Bretagne Hotel.*

WHERE TO STAY

Athens offers an excellent range of accommodation. **Hotels** in Greece are classified in six categories: Luxury, A, B, C, D and E. Generally, luxury hotels cost upwards of 100 for a double room per night, while D and E category hotels charge around 40. Prices are often discounted during the winter low season. Reservations are imperative during the high season (July–August). For a comprehensive list of accommodation in Athens and elsewhere in Greece, visit ⌨ www.greekhotel.com

Camping (usually around 5 per night) is a good budget option in rural areas. However, only use authorized campsites; a list is available at ⌨ www.greecetravel.com/campsites

Self-catering apartments and villas can be booked through a number of travel agents – although the majority concentrate on the Greek islands.

Remember that Athens stays up late so, if your hotel is on a busy, noisy street, it may well be worth requesting a room at the rear – even if you forsake the view.

Pláka, close to many of the city's top sites and offering a wide range of accommodation styles and price categories, is the most popular place to stay – be sure to book well in advance, though, particularly during the high season. If you are having trouble finding a room, try the reservation desk at the **Hotel Association** (*see* side panel).

Hotel Association
✉ 24 Stadíou Street, Syntagma Square
☎ 210 323 7193
📠 301 331 0810
📧 aha@otenet.gr
⌨ http://users.otenet.gr/~aha/
🕐 08:30–14:00 Mon–Thu, 08:30–13:00 Fri, 09:00–13:00 Sat.

Athens

• LUXURY

Andromeda

(off the map)

This immaculate boutique-style hotel is a member of the Small Luxury Hotels of the World. Located in a quiet street behind the concert hall.
⊠ 22 Timoléontos Vássou, Ampelokipoi, ☎ 210 641 5000, 💻 www. andromedaathens.gr

Athenaeum Inter-Continental

(off the map)

A modern hotel with spacious rooms, a health club, pool and rooftop restaurant offering lovely views.
⊠ 89–93 Syngroú, Neos Kosmos, ☎ 210 920 6000, 💻 www. inter-continental.com

Athenian Inn

(Map B–G4)

Located in the heart of Kolonáki's shopping and dining district.
⊠ 22 Cháritos, Kolonáki, ☎ 210 723 8097.

Holiday Inn

(Map B–I4)

Modern hotel with comfortable rooms and a rooftop pool.
⊠ 50 Mihalakopoulou, Ilisia, ☎ 210 727 8000, 💻 www. hiathensgreece.com

Divanis Caravel

(Map B–I5)

Close to the National Gallery, with spacious rooms, a heated pool and a roof garden.
⊠ 2 Vas. Alexándrou, Kaisarianí, ☎ 210 720 7000, 💻 www. divanicaravel.gr

Divani Palace Acropolis

(Map B–D6)

Stylish hotel close to Pláka and the Acropolis.
⊠ 19–25 Parthenónos, Makrigiánni, ☎ 210 928 0100, 💻 www. divaniacropolis.gr

Electra Palace

(Map B–E5)

Offering views of the Acropolis, the Electra has good facilities including a garage and rooftop pool.
⊠ 18 Nikodímou, Pláka, ☎ 210 337 0000.

Grande Bretagne

(Map B–F4)

A city landmark, this former royal palace was modernized in 2002. Superb style and service with a beautiful marble lobby and luxurious rooms.
⊠ Syntagma Square, ☎ 210 333 0000, 💻 www.starwood.com

Hilton

(Map B–H4)

Extensively renovated in 2003, the Hilton boasts superb facilities and stunning views.
⊠ 46 Leofóros Vas. Sofías, Ilisia, ☎ 210 728 1000, 💻 www.hilton.com

Ledra Marriott

(off the map)

All the comforts and amenities of a modern luxury hotel.
⊠ 113–115 Syngroú, Neos Kosmos, ☎ 210 930 0000, 💻 www.marriott.com

Pentelikón

(off the map)

Fine hotel with beautiful rooms, a Michelin-starred restaurant, a garden and pool. Close to the metro.

✉ 66 Diligiánni Street, Kifissiá,

☎ 210 623 06507.

Royal Olympic

(Map B–E6)

Great views of the Temple of Olympian Zeus, plus large rooms, a rooftop bar and excellent restaurant.

✉ 28–32 Diákou, Makrigiánni,

☎ 010 922 6411.

St George Lycabettus

(Map B–G3)

On the slopes of Lykavitós Hill; stunning views, large, modern rooms and a wonderful art collection.

✉ 2 Kleoménous, Kolonáki,

☎ 210 729 0711,

🖥 www.sglycabettus.gr

• MID-RANGE

Achilleas

(Map B–E4)

The top-floor rooms open onto a terrace.

✉ 21 Leka, Pláka,

☎ 210 323 3197.

Acropolis House

(Map B–E5)

Large rooms in a wonderful old pension.

✉ 6–8 Kódrou, Pláka,

☎ 210 322 3244.

Adonis

(Map B–E5)

Modern hotel with roof garden and rooms with balconies and views.

✉ 3 Kódrou, Pláka,

☎ 210 324 9737.

Amalia

(off the map)

Clean, basic rooms; great location opposite National Gardens.

✉ 10 Amalías, Syntagma,

☎ 210 323 7301,

🖥 www.amalia.gr

Aphrodite

(Map B–E4)

Good location with some rooms offering views of the Acropolis.

✉ 21 Apóllonos, Pláka,

☎ 210 323 4357.

Astor

(Map B–E4)

Excellent central location and stunning views from rooftop restaurant.

✉ 16 Karagiórgi Servías, Syntagma,

☎ 210 335 1000.

Cecil

(Map B–D3)

Recently refurbished, well-equipped rooms.

✉ 39 Athinas, Monastiráki,

☎ 210 321 7909.

Ermís

(Map B–E4)

Large rooms and roof garden.

✉ 19 Apóllonos, Pláka, ☎ 210 323 5514.

Kouros

(Map B–E5)

Great location in the heart of Pláka, clean basic rooms in a converted neoclassical mansion.

✉ 11 Kódrou, Pláka,

☎ 210 322 7431.

Iródeion

(Map B–D6)

Modern, comfortable

rooms close to Herodes Atticus Theatre.
✉ *4 Rovértou Gkálli, Makrigiánni,*
☎ *210 923 6832.*

Nefeli
(Map B–E5)
Quiet location with comfortable rooms.
✉ *16 Iperídou, Pláka,*
☎ *210 322 8044.*

Parthenon
(Map B–E6)
Close to metro, clean comfortable rooms, some with views.
✉ *6 Makrí, Makrigiánni,*
☎ *210 923 4594.*

Titánia
(Map B–E2)
A popular rooftop restaurant, good views, well-equipped rooms.
✉ *52 Panepistimíou, Omónia,*
☎ *210 330 0111,*
🖳 *www.titania.gr*

• BUDGET
Faidrá
(Map B–E5)
Basic rooms near Lysikrátous Monument.
✉ *16 Chairefóntos, Pláka,* ☎ *210 323 8461.*

John's Place
(Map B–E4)
Small, clean rooms with shared bathrooms. Ideal location.
✉ *5 Patróou, Pláka,*
☎ *210 322 9719.*

Marble House
(off the map)
Pension with mostly en-suite rooms.
✉ *35 Anastasiou Zinni, Koukáki,*
☎ *210 923 4058.*

Museum
(Map B–E1)
Clean modern rooms with en-suite rooms.
✉ *16 Boumboulinas, Exárchia,*
☎ *210 380 5611.*

Témpi
(off the map)
Good location near metro station, clean hotel popular with students.
✉ *29 Eólou, Monastiráki,*
☎ *210 321 3175.*

Piraeus
• LUXURY
Kastella
(Map F–E2)
Good views of Tourkolímano.
✉ *75 Vas. Pávlou,*
☎ *210 411 4735.*

Cava d'Oro
(Map F–E3)
Comfortable rooms; a popular bar and disco; overlooks harbour.
✉ *19 Vasileos Pávlou,*
☎ *210 412 2210.*

• MID-RANGE
Lilia
(off the map)
A clean and comfortable hotel.
✉ *131 Zéas, Passalimáni,*
☎ *210 417 9108.*

• BUDGET
Achillion
(off the map)
En-suite rooms available at this simple hotel.
✉ *63 Notára,*
☎ *210 412 4029.*

Glyfada
• LUXURY
Oasis
(Map C–F3)
Some apartments overlook the beach. Pools and a jacuzzi.
✉ *27 Poseidónos,*
☎ *210 894 1742.*

• MID-RANGE
Zina
(Map C–F3)
Well-equipped apartments; quiet location.
⊠ 6 Evangelistras,
☎ 210 960 3872.

Vouliagméni
• LUXURY
Aphrodite Astir Palace
(Map C–F3)
Resort hotel with bars, beaches and water sports.
⊠ 40 Apollonos,
☎ 210 890 2000.

Cape Soúnion
• MID-RANGE
Saron
(Map C–F3)
vLovely setting with comfortable rooms.
⊠ 4km (2.5 miles) from the Cape,
☎ 229 203 9144.

Mount Párnitha National Park
• LUXURY
Grand Hotel Mont Parnés
(Map C–E2)
Located at 1050m

(3444ft), this hotel offers sweeping views across Attica.
⊠ Near Ág. Triáda,
☎ 210 246 9111,
⊕ Casino: 07:30–01:45 Thu–Tue.

Delphi
• LUXURY
Xenía
(Map C–C1)
Just 600m (660yd) from Ancient Delphi; large rooms and an indoor pool.
⊠ 69 Apóllonos,
☎ 226 508 2151.

• MID-RANGE
Varónos
(Map C–C1)
Clean, comfortable rooms with balconies.
⊠ 25 Vas. Pávlou,
☎ 226 508 2345.

• BUDGET
Pension Sibylla
(Map C–C1)
Simple, pleasant, well-priced, en-suite rooms.
⊠ 9 Vas. Pávlou,
☎ 226 508 2335.

Apollon Camping
(Map C–C1)
Excellent campsite has a shop, barbecue area,

pool and restaurant.
⊠ 1.5km (1 mile) west of Delphi,
☎ 226 508 2750.

Aegina Town
• LUXURY
Eginitiko Arhontiko
(Map C–E3)
Converted 19th-century mansion.
⊠ Thomaïdou,
☎ 229 702 4968.

• MID-RANGE
Pavlou
(Map C–E3)
Comfortable, family-run guest house.
⊠ 21 Aeginitou,
☎ 229 702 2795.

Póros
• LUXURY
Sirene
(Map C–E4)
This hotel has a pool and private beach.
☎ 229 802 2741.

• MID-RANGE
Seven Brothers
(Map C–E4)
Comfortable, air-conditioned rooms near the waterfront.
⊠ Plateía Iroön,
☎ 229 802 3412.

Hydra Town

• LUXURY
Orloff
(Map C–E4)
Beautiful, 19th-century mansion near the harbour.
☎ 229 805 2564.

• MID-RANGE
Miranda
(Map C–E4)
A lovely town house.
☎ 229 805 2230.

• BUDGET
Hydra
(Map C–E4)
This comfortable hotel offers wonderful views from high above the harbour.
☎ 229 805 2102.

Spétses Town

• LUXURY
Possidonion
(Map C–D4)
Edwardian-style hotel on the waterfront.
☎ 229 807 2308.

• MID-RANGE
Villa Marina
(Map C–D4)
Centrally located, small and friendly.
☎ 229 807 2646.

Ancient Corinth

• MID-RANGE
Shadow
(Map C–D3)
Basic, clean rooms; surrounds the ruins.
☎ 274 103 1232.

Mycenae

• MID-RANGE
La Petite Planete
(Map C–D3)
Comfortable hotel; has a pool and views across orange groves.
☎ 275 107 6240.

• BUDGET
Belle Helene
(Map C–D3)
Small hotel with a modern resturant.
☎ 275 107 6225.

Nafplio

• LUXURY
Ilion
(Map G–A2)
Renovated mansion with lavish facilities.
✉ 6 Kapodistriou,
☎ 275 202 5114.

• MID-RANGE
Byron
(Map G–B2)
Lovely restored rooms, some with views.

✉ 2 Plátanos,
☎ 275 202 2351.

• BUDGET
Dimétris Békas
(Map G–A2)
Well-located in old town with a rooftop terrace offering views.
✉ 26 Efthiopoúlou,
☎ 275 202 4594.

Olympia

• LUXURY
Europa
(Map C–A3)
Modern hotel with hilltop views and excellent facilities.
✉ Ancient Olympia,
☎ 262 402 2650.

• MID-RANGE
Pelops
(Map C–A3)
Small, pleasant family-run hotel.
✉ 2 Vareia,
☎ 262 402 2543.

• BUDGET
Poseidon
(Map C–A3)
Good value pension with clean rooms and a popular bar and restaurant.
✉ 8 Stefanopoulou,
☎ 262 402 2576.

EATING OUT

On the Menu

Taramasaláta: puréed mullet roe and breadcrumbs.

Tzatzíki: yoghurt with cucumber, garlic and mint.

Melitzanosaláta: grilled aubergines and herbs.

Ntolmádes: vine leaves stuffed with rice, pine nuts and currants.

Saganáki: slices of cheese fried in olive oil.

Kotópoulo riganáto: spit-roasted chicken.

Arní me vótana: casserole of lamb on the bone with vegetables and herbs.

Psária plakí: whole fish baked in a vegetable and tomato sauce.

Kalamária: fried squid.

Giaoúrti kai méli: yoghurt with honey.

EATING OUT
What to Eat

Eating out is a highlight of any visit to Athens. In addition to well-known favourites like Greek salad, moussaka and gyros, there is a mouth-watering range of dishes based on local and international cuisine (from sushi to spaghetti). At one extreme, you can dine like an ancient Greek at **Archaion Gefsis** (in Piraeus) which serves huge portions of roast meats and fish – and at the other, you can pop into **McDonalds** (Syntagma Square) for a takeaway burger and fries.

A traditional Greek meal starts with bread and a selection of starters (*mezédes*). These can include anything from *tzatzíki* (cucumber, yoghurt and garlic dip) and *saganáki* (fried cheese) to meatballs and prawns. Sweet Florina peppers, pistachio nuts and, of course, olives also make tasty pre-dinner nibbles.

Main dishes range from herb-rich rural stews like *stifádo* (beef with potatoes and onions) and *arní me vótana* (lamb on the bone with beans and potatoes) to delicious seafood, such as *kalamária* (squid) and prawns. It's worth bearing in mind that

many places start cooking around mid-morning and keep dishes warm until lunch. If you want food piping hot choose something that needs to be freshly cooked such as *souvláki* (meat or fish kebabs) or

Left: Choriátiki *(a salad of tomatoes, cucumber, herbs and feta cheese) and the popular dip,* tzatzíki, *make a classic Greek lunch.*
Opposite: *Tasty trio:* soutzoukákia *(herb-flavoured meat balls) with fried aubergines and tomato salad.*

grilled fish. Remember, too, that Greeks generally eat much later than you may be used to.

Desserts are not often eaten during a main meal. Cakes, puddings and ice cream are usually enjoyed as afternoon snacks after a long siesta. Sweets include *loukoumia* (yeast doughnuts in syrup) and *chalvas* (sweetmeats).

If eating 'on the hoof' between a hectic round of sightseeing is called for, then Athens' numerous street vendors can oblige with tasty **street snacks** like *koulouri* (sesame-seed bread rings), *tyropitta* (cheese pies) and *bougátsa* (custard tarts).

Athens caters for locals eating Greek food at Greek times, as well as tourists seeking familiar food at familiar times. If you want to go Greek, take a light breakfast of yoghurt and honey followed by a mid-morning snack (a cheese pie or sesame seed bread ring). Lunch is late (usually starting around 14:00) and can be a lengthy, highly social affair with wine. Then it's time for the all-important siesta followed by an evening drink and a late dinner at about 22:00. Expect to pay around 10 per person for a typical taverna meal with wine.

Easter Food

Ceremonies and festivities during Greek Orthodox Easter are symbolized by several types of food. Egg loaves containing eggs with red-dyed shells signify the blood of Christ. The end of Lent is celebrated by eating Easter biscuits, while on Easter Sunday lunch often consists of spit-roast lamb accompanied by the first bottles of retsina from the previous year's harvest.

Right: *Traditional Greek coffee is brewed in a long-handled* mpriki *using very finely ground beans.*

What to Drink

Although **beers** and **soft drinks** often accompany meals, the local **wine** industry has begun developing a good reputation and you should look out for leading brands, such as Boutari, Domaine Carras and Kourtakis. By contrast, the famous **retsina** (resinated white wine) will always be an acquired taste – as will the aniseed-flavoured Greek aperitif, **ouzo**.

Popular with the younger 'in crowd', *frappé* is basically iced instant coffee – pale and frothy. By comparison, tradition-al **Greek coffee** is very strong. It is poured from a long-handled *mpriki* and served in a tiny cup.

Where to Eat

You will never go hungry in Pláka and Monastiráki – both districts are riddled with tavernas and bars. Some of the most atmospheric places to eat are along **Adrianoú** (opposite the Ancient Agora), **Plateía Lysikrátous** (overlooking the choregic monument), **Plateía Mitropoleos** (beneath the cathedral), **Anafiótika** (with views across the Ancient Agora) and the

Retsina

Since ancient times, the resin of the Aleppo pine has been added to grape juice during the fermentation process in order to preserve and flavour retsina. Despite advances made by Attica's 'traditional' wine growers, retsina remains a popular drink in Greece. The Mesógeia region of Attica is renowned for its retsina with major producers, such as Kourtákis, owning vine-yards in Markópoulo and Koropí.

streets surrounding the **Roman Agora**. Be aware, however, that some of the top restaurants close down in summer and move to sister properties in the islands.

More trendy bars and places to eat abound in **Kolonáki**. This is the place to come if you want to pose at outdoor cafés with wealthy Athenians (or those pretending to be) – but don't forget your designer sunglasses.

Athenians rarely dine before 22:00 and many restaurant opening times reflect this. Some restaurants, however, open earlier in the evening to cater to tourists.

Street Snacks

Wherever you're walking in Athens there's usually a street food stall nearby. Sesame-seed bread rings are a popular snack, as are roasted chestnuts and honey cakes. For something more substantial, head for the Mitropóleos area of Monastiráki where you will find a mouth-watering array of *souvláki* – meat, fish or vegetables grilled on a skewer and served in a pitta bread.

Attica Wine Tour
The **Attica Wine Growers Association**, ☎ 210 922 3105, organizes tours to vineyards participating in the Wine Roads of Attica programme. Visits to some of the region's archaeological sites are also included on itineraries. More information on Greek wines can be found at 🖥 www.greekwine.gr

---

Below: *Food stalls, like this one selling bread rings, ensure that you'll never go hungry while sightseeing in Athens.*

<table>
</table>

Where to Eat
Tavernas are casual, often family-run, restaurants offering traditional and good-value food and house wines. **Estiatórias** are more sophisticated restaurants with a wider range of dishes and wines.
Psistarias specialize in grills and spit roasts while **psarotavernas** focus on seafood.
    A **medezopolis** offers a range of small meze dishes which, at an **ouzeri**, are washed down with glasses of ouzo.

Below: *Perfect for a 'walking lunch' – souvlaki meat served in a pitta bread.*

Athens
• LUXURY
Aigli Bistrot
Mediterranean-style food served in a great location with outdoor jazz and cinema in summer.
⊠ *Záppeion Gardens,*
☎ *210 336 9363.*

Beau Brummel
Internationally acclaimed French restaurant.
⊠ *19 Ágiou Dimitriou, Kifissiá,*
☎ *210 623 6780.*

Boschetto
Fine Italian food in a garden setting. Excellent wine selection.

⊠ *Evangelismos Park, Kolonáki,*
☎ *210 721 0893.*

Dáfni
A converted neo-classical mansion makes this a great venue for modern Greek dishes, with specialities like swordfish and pork meatballs.
⊠ *4 Lysikrátous, Pláka,*
☎ *210 322 7971.*

Edodi
Small, stylish restaurant in a neoclassical mansion. Exciting haute cuisine and impeccable service.
⊠ *80 Veikou, Koukáki,*
☎ *210 921 3013.*

GB Corner
Renowned for excellent service, this quality restaurant serves Greek and international food.
⊠ *Grande Bretagne Hotel, Syntagma,*
☎ *210 333 0000.*

Ideal
Established in 1922. A tasty and varied

range of Greek and international cuisine with many specialities.
✉ 46 Panepistimíou, Omónia,
☎ 210 330 3000.

Interni

Designer restaurant serving Italian-Asian fusion cuisine.
✉ 152 Ermoú, Gazi,
☎ 210 346 8900.

Kiku

The place in Athens to eat Japanese sushi. Pricey but stylish.
✉ 12 Dimokrítou, Kolonáki,
☎ 210 364 7033.

Pil Poule

Classy restaurant with stunning Acropolis views and fine wine list. Trendy Mediterranean dishes with strong French influence.
✉ 51 Apostólou Pávlou, Thissio,
☎ 210 342 3665.

Spondí

Greek food with a modern twist, extensive wine list and fine desserts. Lovely

neoclassical mansion with courtyard for summer dining.
✉ 5 Pyrronos, Pangrati,
☎ 210 756 4021.

Symposio

Delicious modern Greek food served in the garden or conservatory of a neoclassical mansion. Try the signature dish of fish baked in a salt crust.
✉ 46 Herodeio, Makrigiánni,
☎ 210 922 5321.

• MID-RANGE
Cellier Le Bistrot

Extensive wine list and a good range of light meals make this a good lunch venue.
✉ 10 Panepistimíou, Syntagma,
☎ 210 363 8535.

Eden

Long-established vegetarian restaurant using organic produce.
✉ 12 Lysíou, Pláka,
☎ 210 324 8858.

Kallimármaron

Located near the old Olympic stadium, this

Above: *Olives come in many sizes, shapes and colours, cured in brine, salt, water or oil.*

All About Olives
Ancient Greeks believed the olive tree was a gift from the gods. Not only did they start clearing the country's native forest to grow olive plantations, but in the 6th century BC Solon introduced a death sentence to anyone convicted of cutting down one of the sacred trees. Today, there are some 130 million cultivated olive trees in Greece, producing the world's greatest variety of olives – from fat, juicy Ionian green olives to sweet, dark Kalamátas varieties. Following harvest, olives are either pressed to make oil or preserved in brine, oil, salt or water.

Above: *Tavernas, like this one in Pláka, are often family-run and offer traditional Greek dishes.*

Vegetarian Options
Most restaurants and tavernas provide plenty of choice for vegetarians, both for starters and main courses. As well as the ubiquitous Greek salad, try dishes such as *melitzánes imám baïldí* (aubergines stuffed with onions, tomatoes and herbs) or *fasoláda* (kidney beans baked with vegetables, herbs and olive oil). The most renowned vegetarian restaurant in Athens is the **Eden**, ✉ 12 Lyssiou, Pláka, ☎ 210 324 8858, ⏰ 12:00–24:00 Wed–Mon , which uses soya to create vegetarian versions of old favourites, like moussaka.

---

family-run taverna serves traditional Greek dishes.
✉ 13 *Eforionos, Pangrati,*
☎ *210 701 9727.*

Nefeli

Taverna and coffee shop next to the Ancient Agora, serving lunch and dinner.
✉ 24 *Pános, Pláka,*
☎ *210 321 2475.*

O Mpókaris

Renowned taverna with excellent grills and pies.
✉ 17 *Sokrátous, Kifissiá,*
☎ *210 801 2589.*

Platanos

Long-established taverna near Lysikrátous Monument.
✉ 4 *Diogénis, Pláka,*
☎ *210 322 0666.*

Stavlos

Situated in old Royal Stables. Bar and restaurant with art gallery.
✉ 10 *Irakleidon, Thissio,*
☎ *210 346 7206.*

Terína

Lovely location in Agorás Square, good taverna food.
✉ 25 *Kapnikaréas, Pláka,*
☎ *210 321 5015.*

Zidoron

Popular eatery renowned for its delicious *mezédes*.
✉ 10 *Táki, Psirrí,*
☎ *210 321 5368.*

• **BUDGET**
Athinaikón

Long-established and popular restaurant with lots of atmosphere and a good menu of *mezédes* and seafood dishes.
✉ 2 *Themistokléous, Omónia,*
☎ *210 383 8485.*

Diporto

Basement taverna serving simple but delicious traditional fare.
✉ 9 Sokrátous, Monastiráki,
☎ 210 321 1463.

Ouzeri Kouklis

An old favourite of locals and tourists alike. *Mezédes*, wine and ouzo.
✉ 14 Tripodon, Pláka,
☎ 210 324 7605.

Strofi

Stunning rooftop views guarantee the popularity of this traditional taverna.
✉ 25 Rovértou Gkálli, Acropolis,
☎ 210 921 4130.

Taki 13

Great atmosphere with live music (jazz, blues or Greek). Simple, but tasty range of *mezédes*.
✉ 13 Taki, Psirrí,
☎ 210 325 4707.

Taverna Barbargiannis

Delicious daily specials are chalked up on the blackboard inside this popular taverna.
✉ 94 Emmanuel Benáki, Exárchia,
☎ 210 330 0185.

Taverna tou Psirrí

Hearty Greek cuisine with dishes taking their inspiration from the owner's home island of Náxos.
✉ 12 Aischylou, Psirrí,
☎ 210 321 4923.

Taverna Vicantino

Popular with locals, this taverna serves all the traditional favourites.
✉ 18 Kydathineon, Pláka,
☎ 210 322 7368.

Thanasis

Excellent souvlakia to take away or eat there.
✉ 69 Mitrópoleos, Monastiráki,
☎ 210 324 4705.

To Steki tou Elia

Renowned for lamb chops, but also serves excellent steaks and salads.
✉ 5 Epahalkou, Thissio,
☎ 210 345 8052.

Piraeus
• LUXURY
Istioploikos

Fresh seafood on a moored ship in the harbour.
✉ Tourkolímano (Mikrolímano),
☎ 210 413 4084.

Jimmy the Fish

Taverna along the waterfront at Tourkolímano; excellent seafood – lobster spaghetti a speciality.
✉ 46 Akti Koumoundourou,
☎ 210 412 4417.

Varoúlko

An excellent seafood taverna using local ingredients in wonderfully creative dishes.
✉ 14 Deligorgi,
☎ 210 411 2043.

• MID-RANGE
Archaion Gefsis

Eat like an ancient Greek in this atmospheric and fun themed restaurant. Specialities include roast meats and pureéd vegetables.
✉ 10 Epidavrou,
☎ 210 413 8617.

Margaró

Seafood taverna, popular with locals and tourists alike.
✉ 126 Hatzikyriákou,
☎ 210 451 4226.

Alli Skála

Traditional dishes served in a courtyard filled with banana trees.
✉ 57 Serifou,
☎ 210 482 7722.

Glyfada

• *MID-RANGE*

Far East

Excellent Chinese restaurant with a reputation for delicious Peking duck.
✉ Lazaraki and Pandoras,
☎ 210 894 0500.

• *BUDGET*

O Tzórtzis

Taverna serving tasty traditional food.
✉ 4 Konstantinou-póleos,
☎ 210 894 6020.

Vári

• *MID-RANGE*

Ta Vlachika

Specialize in meat grills and renowned for their delicious spit-roasted lamb and suckling pig.
✉ 35 Leofóros Váris,
☎ 210 895 6141.

Vouliagméni

• *LUXURY*

Lámpros

Waterside restaurant offering fine seafood and an excellent wine list.
✉ 20 Leofóros Poseidónos,
☎ 210 896 0144.

Mt Párnitha National Park

• *MID-RANGE*

O Vlachos

Located in the foot-hills, this Greek taverna has a good selection of meat grills.
✉ Leoforos Parnithos,
☎ 210 246 3762.

Delphi

• *MID-RANGE*

Taverna Váchos

An excellent taverna serving all the old favourites.
✉ 31 Apóllonos,
☎ 226 508 3186.

Saronic Gulf Islands

The harbour at Aegina Town has plenty of cafés and restaurants with good seafood tavernas near the fish market. Póros Town has a great selection of tavernas. Try **Karavolos**, **Platanos**, **Caravella** and **The Flying Dutchman**. Hydra Town has a plethora of places to eat. Try **Xeri Elia** and **To Kryfo Limani**. The old harbour on Spétses has some excellent seafood tavernas, including **Exedra**, **Liotrivi** and **Tarsanas**.

Peloponnese

Ancient Corinth has limited places to eat, although a couple of tavernas worth seeking out are **Marinos** and **Tassos**. The modern settlements near the ancient ruins of Mycenae and Olympia tap into the passing coach tour trade with a spattering of restaurants and cafés. In Nafplio, however, you are spoilt for choice. There is a line of restaurants along Bouboulínas overlooking the port, plus lots more tucked into the old town and around the squares. The following tavernas all come highly recommended:

O Vasílis, **To Fanária**, and **Zorbás**, all on Staïkopoúlou; **Poseidon** and **Tou Stelára** on Bouboulínas.

Cafés and Coffee Shops in Athens
Brazil Coffee Shop
Range of coffees, plus cakes and pastries.
⊠ 1 Voukourestiou, Syntagma,
☎ 210 323 5463.

Dodoni
Ice cream galore.
⊠ 9 Milioni, Kolonáki,
☎ 210 363 7387.

Filion
Copious cakes.
⊠ 34 Skoufa, Kolonáki,
☎ 210 361 2850.

Kotsolis
Traditional sweets and pastries.
⊠ 112 Adrianoú, Pláka,
☎ 210 322 1164.

To Tistrato
Tea, coffee and desserts.
⊠ Corner of Aggelou Geronta and Dedalou, Pláka,
☎ 210 324 4472.

Varsos
Historic patisserie dating back to 1892. Mouth-watering range of sweets and pastries, plus excellent coffee.
⊠ 5 Kassaveti, Kifissiá,
☎ 210 801 3743.

> **Cafés and Coffee Shops**
> **Kolonáki Square** has a reputation for the best **coffee** in Athens, but there are also plenty of **cafés** throughout the city offering everything from strong Greek coffee to ice-cream and traditional pastries and sweets.

Below: *Drying octopuses on the island of Spetses.*

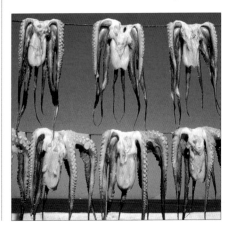

Right: *Enjoying tasty traditional food in one of the city's many bars is a great way to spend an evening out.*

Calendar of Events
• **6 January – Epiphany:** Blessing of the waters at Piraeus where men dive into the sea to retrieve a cross.
• **February – Carnival:** Music, dance and fancy-dress parades in Pláka.
• **February/March – Ash Monday:** Kites are flown from city hills.
• **25 March – Independence Day:** Military or school parade celebrating the Greek uprising against Turkish occupation.
• **1 May – Labour Day:** Workers' parades.
• **Summer – Athens Festival and Epidaurus Festival:** Music, drama and dance at historical theatres in Athens and the Peloponnese.
• **July – Rockwave:** A three-day rock music festival.
• **28 October – Óchi Day:** Military parade in honour of General Metaxas who rejected Mussolini's request for Italian troops to use Greek ports with a terse '*Óchi*' ('No').

ENTERTAINMENT
Nightlife

Athens boasts an exciting range of bars, clubs, music and dance venues, festivals and theatre. English-language listings can be found in the daily *Kathimerini* supplement (in the *International Herald Tribune*), the weekly *Athens News* and the quarterly *Welcome to Athens* (available from the tourist office).

Music

Music runs in the Greek blood. Everything from folk to rock can be sampled at various venues during the summer. **Rembetika** – a kind of Greek Blues – is a hybrid of traditional Greek music and mellow overtones introduced by homesick immigrants from

Asia Minor. One of the most popular of the Greek traditional instruments, the bouzouki belongs to the lute family. It is plucked with a plectrum and is often used to play traditional Rembetika music. An evening at one of Athens' Rembetika bars can be highly atmospheric.

Boasting superb acoustics, the state-of-the-art **Mègaron Musikís Concert Hall** features a range of classical performances, from opera to classical concerts – Greek and international. Music recitals are also sometimes held in the gardens of the **Museum of Greek Popular Musical Instruments** (*see* page 36). During the **Epidaurus Festival** (*see* page 74) musical performances take place at Epidaurus' **Mikro Theatre**.

Lykavitós Theatre is an open-air theatre on Lykavitós Hill where classical, jazz and rock concerts are held during summer. The **Greek National Opera** hosts performances at the **Olympia Theatre** and the **Acropol Theatre**.

Son et Lumière

A popular tourist activity, the sound and light show is held in English at the **Hill of the Pnyx Theatre** (*see* side panel). During the show, music and narration accompany a mesmerizing play of light across the monuments of the Acropolis.

Moonlight Concerts

Key archaeological sites in Athens are opened to visitors during the full moon in September – a magical experience on a clear night. Moonlight concerts are also held in the Roman Agora. For more information check ⌨ www.culture.gr

---

Music Venues:
Mègaron Musikís Concert Hall (Athens Concert Hall)
✉ 89 Vas. Sofias, Illissia
☎ 210 728 2333
🖥 www.megaron.gr
✆ tickets@megaron.gr
🍴 Allegro Restaurant
☎ 210 728 2602/3

Mikro Theatre
✉ Epidaurus
☎ 210 728 2333
🕐 July

Lykavitós Theatre
✉ Lykavitós Hill
☎ 210 722 7233
📠 210 722 7209

Olympia Theatre
✉ 59 Akadimías
☎ 210 361 2461
🖥 www.nationalopera.gr
✆ info@nationalopera.gr
🕐 Nov–Jun

Acropol Theatre
✉ 9–11 Ippokratus Street
☎ 210 364 3700

Hill of the Pnyx Theatre
✉ Off Dionysiou Areópagitou
☎ 210 322 1459
🕐 Starting at 21:00, nightly

Theatres
Amore Theatre
Central Stage
✉ 10 Prigiponisson Street, Athens
☎ 210 646 8009
🖳 www.amorenotos.com
🖉 info@amorenotos.com

Anihto Theatre
✉ 70 Kalvou Street. (corner of Gyzi Street), Athens
☎ 210 644 5749

Experimental Stage of National Theatre
✉ 24–26 Ágiou Konstantinou Street (garage entrance: 28 Koumoundourou Street), Athens
☎ 210 528 8138, 5223242, 52 3322

Greek National Theatre
✉ 24–26 Ágiou Konstantinou Street
☎ 210 528 8100
📠 210 522 5037
🖳 www.n-t.gr/nautilus/5/index.html
🖉 n-t@n-t.gr

Schedia Theatre
✉ 34 Voutadon Street, Gazi, Athens
☎ 210 347 7448
🖳 www.schedia.gr
🖉 schedia@schedia.gr

Opposite: *Dancers often dress in brightly coloured traditional costumes.*

Theatre

Athens has a lively **drama** scene dating from the 6th century BC when the **Dionysia Festival** took place.

An annual five-day theatrical contest, Great Dionysia was a highlight in the social calendar of ancient Athens. On day one, participants paraded hundreds of cows and bulls destined to be sacrificed to the god, Dionysos. His cult statue was brought from Eleutherai to watch the proceedings. On the second day, Athens' allies made tributes of silver, treaties were announced and special honours accorded before the theatrical plays began. These consisted of tragedies and satires until the final day when comedies were performed. Well over a thousand men and boys took part in the plays each year.

Today, the works of great playwrights such as Aeschylus, Aristophanes, Euripides and Sophocles are still performed – along with contemporary ballet and theatre (*see* side panel for theatres). Most theatre performances are, however, in Greek. During the Epidaurus Festival classic Greek dramas are staged by the **Greek National Theatre** (*see* side panel).

Dance

The internationally-acclaimed **Dóra Strátou** traditional folk dance troupe perform at the **Dóra Strátou Dance Theatre** (*see* panel, opposite page). The amazing performance runs for aproximately 80 minutes.

Cinema

Mainstream cinemas in Athens showing films with Greek subtitles, include the **Apollon &**

Attikon Renault, the Elly, and the Ideal. A major highlight for cinema-goers is the annual **Athens film festival** (see page 74).

Festivals
Athens Festival
From June–September, the **Theatre of Herodes Atticus** (see page 24) is the magnificent historical venue for the **Athens Festival** – a showcase for classical and contemporary musicians, actors and dancers from around the world.

Ancient Greek dramas are also performed at other venues, such as the **Lycabettus Theatre** (see panel on page 71) and the **Ancient Theatre of Epidaurus** (see panel on page 74). Programme information and tickets are available from the Central Box Office (see panel on page 74).

Dóra Strátou
✉ Scholiou 8, Philopáppou Hill, Pláka
☎ 210 324 4395 (09:00–16:00) and 210 921 4650 (from 19:30)
🖥 www.grdance.org
✉ mail@grdance.org
🕐 21:30 Tue–Sat, 20:15 Sun, summer
💰 €13
Ⓜ Akropolis

Cinemas
Aigli
✉ Záppeion Gardens, Syntagma
☎ 210 336 9369

Apollon & Attikon Renault Cinema
✉ 19 Stadíou
☎ 210 323 6811

Cine Pari
✉ 22 Kydathineon, Pláka
☎ 210 322 2071

Dexameni
✉ Lykavitós hill, Kolonáki
☎ 210 360 2363

Elly Cinema
✉ 64 Akadimías
☎ 210 363 2789

Ideal Cinema
✉ 46 Panepistimíou
☎ 210 382 6720

Thisseion
✉ 7 Apostolou Pavlou, Thissio
☎ 210 342 0864

Right: *An impressive feature of Ancient Olympia in the Peloponnese, the palaestra was a training centre for boxers, wrestlers and jumpers.*

Festivals:
Hellenic Festival S.A.
Organizes the Athens Festival and Epidaurus Festival.
✉ 23 Hadjihristou and Makriyanni streets
☎ 210 928 2900
📠 210 928 2933
🖳 www. hellenicfestival.gr
🖰 pr@greekfestival.gr

Athens Festival
✉ Theatre of Herodes Atticus (see page 24)
🕘 Jun–Sep
M Akropoli

Epidaurus Festival
✉ Ancient Theatre of Epidaurus, Peloponnese
🕘 weekends in July and August (performances 21:00, Fri and Sat)

Central Box Office
✉ 39 Panepistimíou Street
☎ 210 322 1459
🕘 8:30-16:00 Mon–Fri, 9:00–14:30 Sat

Athens Film Festival
✉ Apollon & Attikon Renault Cinema (see page 73)
☎ 210 606 1413
🖳 www.aiff.gr
🕘 Sep

The Epidaurus Festival

The Epidaurus Festival takes place in July and August. Classic Greek **dramas** are staged by the Greek National Theatre at the **Ancient Theatre of Epidaurus**. Details are available from the box office (*see* side panel).

In July, musical performances take place at Epidaurus' **Mikro Theatre** (*see* page 71).

The Athens Film Festival

The annual **Athens Film Festival** takes place in September. Watching a film at an outdoor cinema is a wonderful way to spend a summer evening. Some of the most popular venues include **Cine Pari** (a rooftop cinema), **Aigli** in the Záppeion Gardens, **Dexameni** on Lykavitós hill and **Thisseion** (*see* panel on page 73 for cinemas).

The Olympic Games

Dismissed as a pagan cult, the games were banned in 393AD by Emperor Theodosius and were not reinstated until 1896 when the first modern Olympic Games were held in Athens. In 2004, the city once again hosts the premier sporting event that has come to embody world peace through the Olympic Truce. Taking place from 13–29 August 2004, the competition schedule includes 28 Olympic sports held at 37 venues.

The first Olympic Games were held every four years (or olympiad) at **Ancient Olympia** (*see* page 83) from as early as 776BC. Dedicated to the gods, they originally had a religious focus with many of the sporting events based on ancient Greek myths. Men from all corners of the ancient Greek world came to compete. Victory was rewarded with an olive wreath – not to mention considerable prestige and power.

Olympics 2004 Developments

Athens' successful bid for the 2004 Olympics led to a welcome injection of investment in and around the capital. In addition to the opening of **Elefthérios Venizélos International Airport** in 2001, developments have included 120km (75 miles) of new highways, extended suburban and light rail links, a 24km (15-mile) tram network, Europe's most modern metro system, new sports and recreational complexes, landscaped pedestrian walkways unifying Athens' archaeological and major cultural sights, a Green Spaces programme, waste management and recycling initiatives, and the introduction of environmentally-friendly transportation vehicles.

The Olympic Stadium
Originally built in 1982 for the 1996 Olympic games (that went to Atlanta), the 78,000-seat Olympic Stadium has been biding its time as Athens' premier soccer venue until it takes centre stage for the 2004 Olympics. Revamped with state-of-the-art touches, such as temperature-regulating ponds and a special roof designed to admit light but not heat, the Olympic Stadium will stage the athletics events, as well as the opening and closing ceremonies. Nearby, as part of the Olympic Sports Complex, are additional facilities for swimming, gymnastics, basketball, cycling, tennis and water polo.
✉ Maroússi, a northern suburb of Athens

The Olympic Committee
Provides information on the 2004 Olympic Games.
☎ 210 200 4000
🖳 www.athens.olympic.org

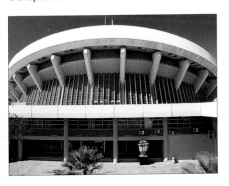

Left: *The Olympic Stadium is part of the Athens Olympic Sports Complex in Maroussi. It is one of the many sporting venues that will be 'upgraded' for the 2004 Olympic Games.*

Spectator Sports

The Greeks have a passion for spectator sports, whether it is watching or betting on the game. **AEK** and **Olympiakos** have strongly supported football, basketball and volleyball teams.

AEK:
⌨ *www.aek.gr/*
Olympiakos:
⌨ *www. olympiacos.org/*

Football

The country's most popular sport is football – the top three teams are Panathinaikos, AEK and Olympiakos. The season runs from September to June and most major matches are played at the Athens Olympic Stadium.

Panathinaikos:
✉ *Apostolos Nikolaidis Stadium, Alexandras Avenue,*
⌨ *www.pao.gr*
AEK:
✉ *Nikos Goumas Stadium, Nea*

Philadelfia,
✏ *football@aek.com*
Olympiakos:
✉ *Rizoupoli Stadium, Piraeus.*

Basketball

Basketball is another popular spectator sport in Greece.
AEK:
✉ *Ano Liosia Stadium*
☎ *302 106856191-5*
✏ *basketball@ aek.com*
Olympiakos:
✉ *Koridalos Stadium*

Volleyball

Volleyball is always entertaining.
AEK:
⌨ *www.aek.gr/*
✏ *volleyball@aek.com*
Olympiakos:
✉ *Glyfada's stadium*

Horse Racing

Horse racing takes place at the Faliro Ippodromo Racecourse.
✉ *Faliro Ippodromo Racecourse, end of Syngrou Avenue,*
☎ *210 941 7761,*
🕐 *17:00 in summer and 15:00 in winter, Mon, Wed, and Fri .*

Nightclubs, Bars and Discos

Banana Moon

A trendy bar and disco.

✉ 1 Vas. Olgas, (next to the old Olympic Stadium, Mets),

☎ 210 752 1768.

Bedlam

A 'cool' new summer bar.

✉ in the Záppeion Gardens, Syntagma,

☎ 210 336 9340.

Brettos

An old-fashioned bar lined with wine barrels and bottles.

✉ 41 Kydathineon, Pláka,

☎ 210 323 2110.

Inoteka

A low-key candlelit bar.

✉ Plateía Avyssinnías, Monastiráki,

☎ 210 324 6446.

Lamda

The gay scene in Athens is centred on the district of Makrigiánni where one of the most popular clubs is Lamda.

✉ 15 Lembesi,

☎ 210 942 4202.

Stavlos

A lively bar with rock music.

✉ 10 Iraklidon, Thissio,

☎ 210 346 7206.

Stoa Athanaton

For the so-called Greek blues, head for this Rembétika club.

✉ 19 Sofokleous, Omónia,

☎ 210 321 4362.

Thirio

A 'happening', often crowded club with loud music.

✉ 2 Lepenioutou, Psirrí,

☎ 210 722 4104.

Nightlife

The districts of Psirrí, Kolonáki and Gazi are the places to go for serious nightlife. However, you will find venues scattered across the capital, ranging from mellow bars to pounding nightclubs. Some only operate between October and April, moving to the coast during summer.

In summer, the cool crowd head for the coast where clubs like **Budha**, in Glyfada, and **Island**, in Varkiza, provide music and drinks by the sea.

Below: *A number of café-bars, such as this one in Pláka, can be found throughout Athens.*

Above: *Unlike the metro, public buses and taxis can fall prey to traffic congestion.*
Opposite: *A wonderful sight as you round a bend on the coastal road from Piraeus: the Temple of Poseidon which crowns Cape Soúnion.*

Best One-day Excursions

• Cruise to the Saronic Gulf island of **Aegina** to visit the temple of Aphaia, one of the best-preserved Doric temples in Greece.
• Drive to **Cape Soúnion** to watch the sun set behind the Temple of Poseidon.
• Join a tour to **Delphi**, once regarded as the spiritual centre of the Greek world.
• Cruise to **Hydra** for a relaxing lunch on the picturesque waterfront.
• Drive to **Corinth** to see the ancient ruins and canal.

EXCURSIONS

Attica, the region surrounding Athens, has plenty to tempt day-trippers from the city. Some of the highlights lie on the outskirts of the capital and can easily be reached by public transport. For others you will need to hire a car or join an organized tour.

Major highways (the E75 and E94) head north and west from Athens towards Thessaloníki and Corinth, respectively. Follow the western route and you will find two historical gems – **Dáfní Monastery** and **Ancient Eleusis**. Most people heading north on a day trip are bound for Delphi. Although well beyond the borders of Attica, the breathtaking combination of mountain scenery and well-preserved ruins more than compensate for the long drive.

Two main routes head south towards the tip of Attica. The most popular follows the coast, passing several beach resorts, to **Cape Soúnion**; another loops inland above Mount Ymittós. South of Athens is the crowded port of **Piraeus** where you can catch a ferry or hydrofoil to the **Saronic Gulf islands**.

Sálamis, Aegina, Hydra, Spétses and **Póros** are the main islands within the Saronic Gulf and are popular holiday haunts for locals and tourists alike. If time is limited, you can join a cruise boat that takes in two or three islands with a few hours spent on each.

Connected to the Greek mainland purely by the bridges that cross the Corinth Canal, the **Peloponnese** makes a superb excursion from Athens. Ancient Corinth, Nafplio, Ancient Mycenae, Epidaurus and Ancient Olympia are all well worth exploring.

Attica South
Piraeus

Lying just 10km (6 miles) from central Athens, Piraeus is one of the biggest ports in the Mediterranean. Most tourists use Piraeus as a transit point for ferries to and from the Saronic islands and beyond. However, the city also offers some interesting museums, impressive architecture and one or two picturesque harbours. Don't expect a laid-back Greek seaside retreat, though – Piraeus is basically Athens-on-sea.

Cape Soúnion

The winding coastal road from Piraeus is a great suspense-builder, hiding Cape Soúnion until you round a final bend and first glimpse the rocky headland with the **Temple of Poseidon** perched on top.

There is no question as to why this site was chosen as a place to worship the mighty god of the sea. Particularly striking at sunset, the Doric temple, dating back to the 5th century BC, commands supreme views across the Aegean.

The path from the tourist centre to the temple crosses the remains of **fortified walls** that were built to protect the cape during the Peloponnesian War. On the west side of the headland are the ruins of ancient **shipyards** that would have sheltered a pair of warships – to safeguard the passage of ships carrying grain to Athens. On a hill slightly inland, 9km (5.5 miles) south of Lávrio, are the remains of the **Sanctuary of Athena Sounias**.

South to the Cape
The enticing, coast-hugging road winding south from Piraeus to Cape Soúnion makes a fascinating excursion that is full of eye-openers – both ancient and modern. Sometimes referred to as the Apollo Coast (after a small temple near Vouliagméni), this route links a chain of popular beaches, lively resorts and quiet coves before culminating in the 'sacred cape' at the southern tip of Attica. It was here that the Athenians built sanctuaries to their two most important deities – Poseidon and Athena.

Piraeus
Location: Map F; C–E3
Distance from Athens: 8km (5 miles)

Cape Soúnion
Location: Map C–F3
Distance from Athens: 75km (47 miles)
Sanctuary of Athena Sounias:
🕐 10:00–sunset, daily

Ancient Eleusis
Location: Map E; C–E2
Distance from Athens:
22km (14 miles) north-
west of Athens
✉ Elefsína
🕐 08:30–15:00 Tue–Sun

Dáfní Monastery
Location: Map C–E2
Distance from Athens:
10km (6 miles) north-
west of Athens
🕐 08:30–15:00, daily

Eleusinian Mysteries
In its heyday, Eleusis
attracted some 30,000
devotees. Secret rituals
took place as part of
the so-called Eleusinian
Mysteries which were
part of a nine-day
annual festival. Initiates
(*mystes*) would present
offerings and purify
themselves before set-
ting off along the
Sacred Way from
Kerameikós to Eleusis.
Little is known about
this most sacred of
ceremonies – hardly sur-
prising considering exe-
cution was the penalty
for spilling the beans.

The Sacred Way

The Sacred Way that once linked Athens
with Eleusis makes a worthwhile excursion,
particularly when combined with the beautiful Byzantine monastery of Dáfní.

Ancient Eleusis

Separated from the Acropolis by modern-
day urban sprawl, Eleusis was once an
intrinsic part of cult worship in ancient
Athens. Founded ca. 2000BC on a hill, its
strategic position led to the development of
a large settlement. Magnificent buildings
embellished the site during Roman and classical periods, but the sanctuary was aban-
doned in the 4th century AD following the
Gothic invasion and spread of Christianity.

Highlights include the site's museum, the
Telesterion, the Greater Propylaia, the
Sacred Court, the Callichoron Well, the
Ploutonion and a pair of triumphal arches.

Dáfní Monastery

Founded in the 5th century AD, this
monastery is built on the site of a sanctuary to Apollo that marked the point where
the Sacred Way began its final approach
to Eleusis. It takes its name from the
laurels (*dáfnes*) that used to grow here.

The **katholikón** (main
church) was built
ca. 1080 and boasts
a dome measuring
8m (26ft) in diameter
and 16m (52ft) high.
Inside the *katholi-
kón* there are some
exquisite gold-leaf
Byzantine mosaics.

Ancient Delphi

Arriving from Aráchova, the first of Delphi's two main sacred areas is the **Sanctuary of Athena Pronaia** (or Marmaria Precinct). Further along is the **Castalian Spring** where the oracle, pilgrims and priests would cleanse themselves prior to any ceremony. The **Sanctuary of Apollo** (or Sacred Precinct) is nearby and contains the ruins of numerous monuments linked by the winding **Sacred Way**. Above the sanctuary is a well-preserved **stadium** while to the west is the **museum** which con-

tains a wealth of statues, friezes and offerings from the Sanctuary of Apollo.

The remains of two **temples** dedicated to the goddess Athena Pronaia can be found at the **Sanctuary of Athena Pronaia**. You will, however, be drawn to the photogenic **Tholos**. This elegant rotunda was built ca. 390BC. Three of its original 20 Doric columns have been re-erected, but the purpose of the building remains a mystery.

The **Sanctuary of Apollo** is riddled with ruins. From the moment you enter, you are in the midst of a **Roman Agora**. From here, the **Sacred Way** climbs past numerous plinths that supported **monuments** to battle victories. Following these are the remains of 27 **treasuries** where offerings and war spoils were held. Next to the **Treasury of the Athenians** is the **Rock of the Sybil** where, according to legend, Delphi's first oracle prophesied. At the top of the Sacred Way, is the **Temple of Apollo** – the most imposing structure at Delphi. Behind the temple is the **theatre** from where beautiful views of Delphi can be enjoyed.

Above: *A chapel at Dáfní Monastery is dedicated to Saint Nicolas.*
Opposite: *Dáfní Monastery, famed for its stunning Byzantine mosaics.*

Ancient Delphi
Location: Map D; C–C1
Distance from Athens: approx. 200km (120 miles)

Archaeological Site and Museum:
✉ Delphi 33054, Phokis, Sterea Hellas
☎ 22650 82312
📠 22650 82966
🖥 www.culture.gr
🕐 07:30–19:00 summer; 08:30–15:00 Mon and 07:30–18:00 Tue–Sun winter
💰 €6 (concessions €3), ticket for museum and site €9 (concession €5), children under 18 free

Above: *Islands like Spétses offer respite from hectic Athens.*

The Saronic Gulf Islands

Aegina

Aegina is a popular seaside destination for Athenians. **Aegina Town**, the island's main port, has a harbour crammed with colourful caïques and lined with cafés and tavernas. North of the town is a small sandy beach, the **Temple of Apollo** and an **Archaeology Museum**; east is the **Temple of Aphaia**; south is a **water park**; and southwest is the **Hellenic Wildlife Rehabilitation Centre**.

Póros

Just 400m (440ft) from the mainland, Póros is really two islands separated by a sandy causeway. **Póros Town** has a small archaeological museum and views across the narrow straits to the Argolid Mountains.

Hydra

Most visitors stay on the waterfront of **Hydra Town** with its wall-to-wall cafés, galleries and jewellery shops. There are some lovely churches, such as the harbourside **Panagía tis Theotókou** while the **Museum of Hydra** looks at the island's seafaring contribution to Greek history.

Spétses

Lying furthest from Athens, Spétses tends to be quieter and more relaxed than other islands in the gulf. The island has some pleasant **beaches**, such as Ágioi Anárgyri and Ágia Paraskeví – both offering water sports. Spétses Town has several **neoclassical mansions** and an **old harbour** with shipyards dating from the 17th century.

Aegina
Location: Map C–E3
Archaeology Museum:
08:30–15:00 Tue–Sun
Water Park:
10:00–20:00, daily
Hellenic Wildlife Rehabilitation Centre:
11:00–13:00, daily
Temple of Aphaia
08:30–17:00 Mon–Fri, 08:30–15:00 Sat and Sun

Póros
Location: Map C–E4

Hydra
Location: Map C–E4

Museum of Hydra:
09:00–16:30 Tue–Sun

Spétses
Location: Map C–D4

The Peloponnese
Corinth

Well-preserved, the ruins of **Ancient Corinth** reveal the Temple of Apollo, an agora, the Léchaion Way, the Temple of Octavia, an odeion and a theatre. The site's **museum** features Roman floor mosaics and early pottery. Above the ruins is the **Acrocorinth** (an impressive acropolis with breathtaking views) while at the summit are the remains of a Temple of Aphrodite.

Argolis

The citadel of **Ancient Mycenae** rears from mountains and ravines. The Cyclopean walls, Lion Gate and Treasury of Atreus are just a few of the impressive sights. The nearby sanctuary of **Epidaurus** contains numerous remains, including a stadium, gymnasium, stoa, temple, 4th century BC hotel, and the best-preserved theatre in Greece.

The elegant city of **Nafplio** is a fusion of airy squares and narrow streets. It contains many craft shops and galleries as well as other places of interest such as Palamídi Fortress, Boúrtzi castle, a Folk Art Museum, War Museum and Archaeological Museum.

Ancient Olympia

Ancient Olympia is a long drive from Athens, but well worth the effort. Highlights include the **stadium**, the **Temple of Hera** and the **Temple of Zeus**. The nearby **Archaeological Museum** showcases the rich finds from Ancient Olympia while the final gallery is devoted to the Olympic Games.

Ancient Corinth
Location: Map C–D3
Distance from Athens: approx. 73km (45 miles)

Ancient Mycenae
Location: Map C–C3
Distance from Athens: approx. 100km (60 miles)

Nafplio
Location: Map C–D4
Distance from Athens: approx. 130km (80 miles)
Palamídi Fortress:
🕐 08:00–19:00 Mon–Fri, 07:30–15:00 Sat, Sun
Folk Art Museum:
🕐 09:00–14:00 Wed–Mon
War Museum:
🕐 09:00–14:00 Tue–Sun
Archaeological Museum:
🕐 08:30–15:00 Tue–Sun

Ancient Olympia
Location: Map H; C–A3
Distance from Athens: approx. 290km (180 miles)
Museum:
🕐 12:00–19:00 Mon, 08:00–19:00 Tue–Sun

Below: *Nafplio is an excellent base from which to explore the eastern parts of the Peloponnese.*

Above: *The Saronic Gulf islands are especially popular during summer when locals escape the heat in Athens.*

Abbreviations
EHS: the urban railway service
ELPA: Touring and Automobile Club of Greece
ELTA: the post office
EOT: the tourist information office
KTEL: the private bus service
OASA/ETHEL: the public bus service
OSE: the railway organization
OTE: the telephone service

Best Times To Visit

Spring and autumn are the best times to visit. Not only is it pleasantly warm and sunny, but the city's main sites and museums will be less crowded. Even as late as November the temperature can be a comfortable 23°C (73°F), while January, the coldest month, usually only drops to a minimum of 12°C (54°F). Winter months, however, are also the wettest (snow is not unheard of). By contrast, summer (June–September) is usually dry with daytime temperatures reaching uncomfortable highs. This is also the most expensive and crowded time to visit.

Tourist Information

The **Greek National Tourist Organisation** (referred to as the **EOT** in Greece) is represented abroad in several countries:
UK, ⊠ 4 Conduit Street, London, W1R 0DJ, ☎ 020 7734 5997, ☏ 020 7287 1369, ☐ www.tourist-offices.org.uk/Greece
USA, ⊠ Olympic Tower, 645 5th Avenue, New York 10022, ☎ 212 421 5777, ☏ 212 826 6940, ☐ www.greektourism.com
Australia, ⊠ 51 Pitt Street, Sydney, NSW 2000, ☎ 02 9241 1663/4/5, ☏ 02 9235 2174.
Canada, ⊠ 1300 Bay Street, Toronto, Ontario M5R 3K8, ☎ 416 968 2220, ☏ 416 968 6533.
In **Athens**, the EOT has offices at ⊠ 2 Amerikis Street, Syntagma, ☎ 210 331 0561, ☐ www. gnto.gr ⏲ 09:00–16:00 Mon–Fri, 10:00–15:00 Sat, and at ⊠ **Elefthérios Venizélos International Airport**, Arrivals Terminal, ☎ 210 353 0445, ⏲ 08:00–22:00 daily. The EOT produces a booklet, *Greece: Athens*, as well as information on a variety of useful topics. The **Tourist Police** can

be contacted ☎ 171, ⏰ 07:00–23:00 daily, to answer (in English) tourist queries or assist with emergencies.

Embassies and Consulates:

Australia, ✉ 37 D. Soútsou, Ambelokipi, ☎ 210 645 0404, ✆ 210 646 6595.

Canada, ✉ 4 Ionna Gennadíou, Evangelismos, ☎ 210 727 3400, ✆ 210 725 3460.

New Zealand, ✉ 268 Kifissías, Halandri, ☎ 210 687 4701, ✆ 210 687 4444.

South Africa, ✉ 60 Kifissías, Maroússi, ☎ 210 610 6645, ✆ 210 610 6636.

UK, ✉ 1 Ploutarchou, Kolonáki, ☎ 210 727 2600, ✆ 210 727 2720.

USA, ✉ 91 Vas. Sofías, Ambelokipi, ☎ 210 721 2951, ✆ 210 645 6282.

Entry Requirements

Visitors from EU countries, Australia, Canada, New Zealand and the USA need only a valid passport for entry into Greece. Citizens of EU countries can stay indefinitely – unless working, in which case a residence permit should be obtained from the Aliens Bureau, ☎ 210 647 6000. Citizens of non-EU countries can stay for up to three months in Greece. Extensions must be applied for at the Aliens Bureau at least 20 days before your initial entry period expires.

Health Requirements

No vaccinations are required for entry into Greece. Emergency medical care is available to EU citizens. However, all visitors are advised to arrange their own comprehensive travel and medical insurance. Prior to travel, UK residents should complete a Form E111 (available from post offices). In theory, this covers the costs of basic treatment, but in Greece you may still be asked to pay up-front in which case you should keep all the receipts in order to make a claim back home.

Getting There

By air: International flights arrive at **Elefthérios Venizélos International Airport**, located 27km (17 miles) northeast of Athens city centre. The following airlines have offices in Athens:

Air Canada, ✉ 8 Zirioi Street, Maroússi, ☎ 210 617 5321;

Air France, ✉ 18 Vouliagménis, Glyfada, ☎ 210 960 1100; **Alitalia**, ✉ 577 Vouliagménis, ☎ 210 998 8888;

American Airlines, ✉ 15 Panepistimíou, ☎ 210 331 1045;

British Airways, ✉ 1 Themistokléos, Glyfada, ☎ 210 890 6666, 🖥 www.ba.com

KLM, ✉ 41 Vouliagménis, Glyfada, ☎ 210 960 5010; **Lufthansa**, ✉ 10 Zirioi, Maroússi, ☎ 210 617 5200;

Olympic Airways, ✉ 96 Syngroú, ☎ 210 966 6666, 🖥 www.

olympic-airways.gr
Singapore Airlines, ✉ 9 Xenofondos, ☎ 210 324 4113; **United Airlines**, ✉ 5 Syngroú, ☎ 210 924 1389.
From the UK, scheduled flights fly direct to Athens with Olympic Airways, British Airways and the no-frills airline Easyjet, ☎ 210 967 0000, 💻 www.easyjet.com
During the summer months Olympic Airways, the national carrier, flies direct to Athens from New York, Boston, Montreal and Toronto.
By rail: To reach Athens by train from London involves taking Eurostar (☎ 0870 160 6600, 💻 www.eurostar.co.uk) to Paris (3 hours) and changing for Brindisi (24 hours). Ferries from Brindisi serve the city of Pátras in the Peloponnese, from where trains operate to Athens. An alternative would be to travel via Venice and board a ferry there.
By road: The best route for **driving** from London to Athens is to take the Eurotunnel ☎ 0870 535 3535, 💻 www.eurotunnel.com across the English Channel before heading south through Reims, Geneva, Milan and on to any of the Italian ferry ports serving Greece (*see* By sea, below for ferry services). Non-EU citizens require an international driving licence. International **buses** link various European capitals with Athens, usually via a ferry crossing from Italy. Operators in London include Busabout, ☎ 020 7950 1661, 💻 www.busabout.com and Eurolines, ☎ 0870 514 3219, 💻 www.gobycoach.com
By sea: Ferries depart from the Italian ports of Ancona, Bari, Brindisi and Venice. There are daily services from Ancona and Brindisi to Pátras. Crossings take 15–20 hours. From Pátras it is a 220km (137-mile) drive to Athens. Ferry operators include: ANEK Lines, ☎ 210 323 3481 and, Superfast Ferries, ☎ 210 331 3252. Bookings for these and other operators can be made at 💻 www.greekferries.gr

What to Pack

For serious sightseeing and museum-browsing you will be grateful for a comfortable pair of shoes. Make sure they have sturdy grips to cope with the uneven and occasionally slippery marble surfaces at archaeological sites. A sun hat, sunglasses and sunblock are also essential. Evenings, even in summer, can be quite chilly, so remember to pack a lightweight jacket or warm sweater. A universal plug for a washbasin may also be useful.

Money Matters

The **euro** (€) replaced the drachma as the currency of Greece in January 2002. Notes are available in 5, 10,

20, 50, 100, 200 and 500 euro denominations, with coins of €1, €2, 50 cents (¢), 20¢, 10¢, 5¢, 2¢ and 1¢. Banks are widespread in Athens (particularly in the Omónia and Syntagma districts). Normal banking times are 08:20–14:00 Mon–Thu, 08:00–13:30 Fri. National Bank of Greece, ✉ Syntagma Square, ⏰ 08:00–14:00 and 15:30–17:30 Mon–Fri, 09:00–15:00 Sat, 09:00–13:00 Sun. There are also banks at the international airport, ⏰ 07:00–21:00. There are numerous 24-hour cash dispensers (ATMs). Credit cards are accepted in most hotels, car rentals and travel agencies, major shops and restaurants. Smaller hotels, shops and tavernas may only take cash.

Currency exchange: Travellers cheques are widely accepted (you will need your passport as proof of ID when cashing them).

Transport

Greece has a comprehensive public transport system. Getting around in Athens or exploring further afield is cheap and straightforward.

Air: Olympic Airways (see Getting There, page 85) operates most domestic flights. The baggage allowance is 15kg (33lb). Popular destinations from Athens include Santorini, Mikonos, Rhodes, Crete, Thessaloníki, and around 30 other islands and mainland cities. Most flights take 50–60 minutes. Airport tax of 12 is included in the price for domestic flights.

Rail: The Greek Railway Organisation (OSE) is gradually updating its rolling stock, although train travel can still be painfully slow. It is, however, incredibly cheap, with the 5-hour route from Athens–Pátras costing around 8 first class. Schedules and fares

Special Needs
Despite an ongoing programme of facilities for the mobility impaired, Athens can be a challenge for wheelchair users. Most major museums and hotels are wheelchair-friendly, but restaurants (often with downstairs toilets) and archaeological sites (with uneven surfaces) can prove difficult. The international airport has excellent provision for disabled travellers, while the metro system (with lifts to the platforms) and the growing number of pedestrianized streets make getting around easier.

Language

Tour guides speak English, French, German and other European languages. Most museums and archaeological sites have at least some interpretation (leaflets, signage etc) in English. Greeks will appreciate any attempt you make to speak even a few words and phrases of their language (see panel, page 91). If you are really serious, consider enrolling at a language school in Athens. Contact the tourist office for more details.

The Athens Centre

Offers Greek language courses for beginners.
✉ 48 Arhimidous (in the Athenian suburb of Mets)
☎ 210 701 2268

Tipping

Although a service charge is included in restaurant bills, it is customary (but not obligatory) to leave a small tip of around 10–15%. Taxi drivers, porters and cloakroom attendants will also appreciate a small gratuity of loose change.

can be found at 🖥 www.ose.gr or ☎ 210 529 7777. The **metro** is the best way to travel across the capital, with three main lines providing access to most major sites, as well as locations in Greater Athens, such as Piraeus and Kifissiá.

Bus: The regional bus service (KTEL, 🖥 www.ktel.org) operates a comprehensive network of efficient services between all main centres. In Athens, blue and white **suburban buses** and overhead cable **trolley buses** operate from 05:00–24:00. A map showing routes can be obtained from the EOT (see page 84), while tickets can be purchased from transport kiosks or news stands (peGraferaptera).

Car: Driving in Athens is not for the faint-hearted. Preserve your sanity by travelling to the city's sites using the metro, buses, taxis or by

walking. If you need independence for exploring further afield, consider taking a bus to the international airport and collecting a **rental car** from there. The following companies all have offices both in the city and at the airport: **Avis**, ✉ 48 Amalias, ☎ 210 322 4951 or 210 353 0578; **National**, ✉ 58–60 Spiroupatsi, ☎ 210 346 3588 or 210 353 3323; **Europcar**, ✉ 4 Syngrou, ☎ 210 924 8810 or 210 353 0580; **Hertz**, ✉ 12 Syngrou, ☎ 210 922 0102 or 210 353 4900; **Sixt**, ✉ 23 Syngrou, ☎ 210 922 0171 or 210 353 0576. The minimum driving age is 18 years. Speed limits are 50kph (30mph) in built-up areas, 120kph (75mph) on highways and 90kph (60mph) on other roads. Seat belts must be worn and there are heavy penalties for driving under the influence of alcohol. Road distances from Athens to Corinth, Nafplio, Pátras and Thessaloniki are 84km (52 miles), 165km (102 miles), 220km (137 miles) and 513km (319 miles) respectively.

Ferry: The two main hubs for ferry transport throughout Greece are Piraeus (south of Athens) and Rafína (on the east coast of Attica). Schedules, fares and booking information are available at 🖳 www.greekferries.gr Hydrofoils are generally twice as fast as ferries – but cost about twice as much.

Travel Passes: In Athens, daily 24-hour travel passes for around €3 are available for use on buses, trolley buses and metro.

Business Hours

Shops are generally open ⏱ 09:00–15:00 Mon and Wed, 09:00–19:00 Tue, Thu and Fri, 08:30–15:30 Sat, closed Sun. Tourist shops and department stores often stay open longer. For opening times of **archaeological sites** and **museums**, refer to individual attractions. Normal hours, however, are usually 08:00 or 09:00 to 14:00 or 15:00 Tue–Sun, closed Mon. **Churches** and **monasteries** often close for a few hours during the middle of the day. **Banks** are open ⏱ 08:20–14:00 Mon–Thu, 08:00–13:30 Fri, while **kiosks** (*periptera*) are open early until late.

Time Differences

Athens is Greenwich Mean Time (GMT) +2, Central European Time +1 and North American Eastern Standard Time +7. Clocks go forward one hour from the last Sunday in March until the last Sunday in October.

Communications

Post offices (*tachidromío*) are easily identified by bright yellow signs. In Athens, the main ones are at ✉ Syntagma Square and ✉ 100 Eolou, Omónia, ⏱ 07:30–20:00 Mon–Fri, 07:30–14:00 Sat, 09:00–13:00 Sun. Stamps (*grammatósima*) are also sold at kiosks and tourist shops (but often with a 10% surcharge). Postcards and letters take up to seven days to reach the UK and 11 days to Australia and the USA. Express service ensures three-day delivery within the EU. Phone cards (*télekartas*) can be purchased at kiosks for use in public **telephones** which allow local and international calls. Press the 'I' (information) button for user instructions in English. To **phone abroad from Greece**, dial 00, followed by the country code, then the city or area code (without the 0 before it) and then the number. To **phone Greece from abroad**, dial the country code 30, then the full 10-digit number. In Athens, standard numbers begin with 2, mobile numbers with 6. **Faxes** and **telegrams** can be sent from post offices. Greece has three **mobile phone** service providers – CosmOTE, Panafon and Telstet. Mobile phones can be rented from 🖳 www.greecetravel.com/phones

Internet and **email** can be accessed from some hotels, as well as several Internet cafés in Athens such as **Astor Internet Café**, ✉ 27 Oktovriou (Patissíon), Omónia, 🕑 10:00–22:00 daily; **Pláka Internet World**, ✉ 29 Pandrosou, Monastiráki, 🕑 11:00–23:00 daily; **Sofokleous.com Internet Café**, ✉ 5 Stadíou, Syntagma, 🕑10:00–22:00 Mon–Sat, 13:00–21:00 Sun.

Electricity

The current in Greece is 220V, 50Hz. Plugs are continental two-pin. Buy adapters at electrical stores or large airports.

Weights and Measures

Greece follows the metric system. Commas are used to indicate decimals, while points are used for thousands. Liquids are often sold by weight rather than volume.

Health Precautions

Although bottled water is widely available, Athens' tap water is safe to drink. During hot summer days, drink plenty of fluids to avoid dehydration and heat exhaustion. Do not underestimate the severity of the sun in Greece. Protect yourself from sunburn by wearing a hat and applying a high factor sunscreen. Also be wary of the black-spined sea urchins along stretches of rocky coast.

Personal Safety

Athens is a safe city. Take normal precautions, such as leaving your passport, tickets and valuables in a hotel safe and carrying small amounts of cash and a credit card in a money belt. Be especially vigilant of pickpockets on the metro and at flea markets. Like any large city there are one or two places to be wary of travelling alone at night. If in doubt, seek local advice or stick to popular tourist areas like Pláka. Be wary of 'scam artists' – usually effusively-friendly men approaching you in the street or in bars, offering to buy you a drink.

Emergencies

Police, ☎ 100, **ambulance**, ☎ 166; **fire brigade**, ☎ 199. For information about the **emergency hospitals**, ☎ 106. **Hospitals: Evangelismos** (public), ✉ 45–47 Ipsilantou,

Kolonáki, ☎ 210 720 1000, **Athens Euroclinic** (private), ✉ 9 Athanasiadou, Ambelokipi, ☎ 210 641 6600. **SOS-Doctors**, ☎ 1016, is a 24-hour service that charges a fixed rate for hotel visits. Although most **pharmacies** are open during normal business hours, a list of after-hours duty pharmacies is published in *Athens News*. The international airport has a permanent 24-hour pharmacy.

Etiquette

A polite greeting – *kaliméra* (good day) or *kalispéra* (good evening) – always goes down well with shop owners, waiters and the like. Other social etiquette to be aware of in Greece is that personal questions are not considered rude. Greeks also believe in the evil eye (bad luck as a result of someone's envy), so if, for example, you compliment the beauty or intelligence of a child, remember to ward off evil spirits by making a ritual 'spitting' sound afterwards. Dress respectfully inside churches and monasteries (covered arms, long trousers or skirts below knees) and make a small donation or buy a candle. Finally, help protect the natural and cultural heritage of Greece by using water sparingly and resisting any temptation to pocket bits of carving or pottery from ancient sites.

Useful Contacts

Airport information: ☎ 210 353 0000, 24hr-a-day for flight information available in both Greek and English.

Left luggage: Pacific Travel, ✉ 26 Nikis, Pláka, ☎ 210 324 1007 and also at the airport near gate 1 on Arrivals, ☎ 210 353 0160.

Useful Phrases

Good morning
• *Kaliméra*
Good evening
• *Kalispéra*
Hello • *Yásas*
Goodbye • *Andío*
Please • *Parakaó*
Thank you • *Evcharistó*
No • *Óchi*
Yes • *Né*
How are you?
• *Ti kánete?*
Where is…?
• *Poo eene…?*
How much?
• *Póso káni?*
What is that?
• *Ti íne aftó*
Do you speak English?
• *Milate Anglika?*
I don't understand
• *Then katalavéno*

Driving

Exit • *Éxothos*
Entrance • *Ísothos*
Slow • *Argá*
No parking
• *Apagorévete ee státhmevsis*
Where is the road to…?
• *Poo eene o thrómos yía…?*
Where can I buy petrol? • *Poo boró n'agorásso venzíni?*

INDEX OF SIGHTS

GENERAL INDEX

Page numbers given in **bold** type indicate photographs

GENERAL INDEX

GENERAL INDEX

GENERAL INDEX